W. H. HUDSON

AMS Studies in Modern Literature, No. 16

ISSN 0270–2983

Other titles in this series:

W. H. HUDSON

THE MAN, THE NOVELIST, THE NATURALIST

Amy D. Ronner

AMS PRESS
NEW YORK

Library of Congress Cataloging-in-Publication Data

Ronner, Amy D.
  W.H. Hudson: the man, the novelist, the naturalist.

  (AMS studies in modern literature; no. 16)
  Revision of the author's dissertation.
  Bibliography: p.
  Includes index.
  1. Hudson, W.H. (William Henry), 1841–1922.
2. Authors, English—19th century—Biography.
3. Naturalists—England—Biography. I. Title.
II. Series.
PR6015.U23Z824 1986   828'.809 (B)   85-48068
ISBN 0-404-61586-4

AMS PRESS, Inc.
56 East 13th Street
N. Y., NY 10003, U.S.A.

Contents

Preface

HEMINGWAY'S Robert Cohn is considered defective because he has been reading W.H. Hudson. It is his obsession with *The Purple Land* that eventually excludes him from the Jake Barnes clique: "For a man to take it at thirty-four as a guide-book to what life holds is about as safe as it would be for a man of the same age to enter Wall Street direct from a French convent, equipped with a complete set of the more practical Alger books." The gauchos, villains, heroines compel Cohn to take off for South America in quest of romance while his cronies plan to drink their way through Spain.

In some American literature course in the middle of a hot summer in Ann Arbor, Michigan, a professor initiated his discussion of *The Sun Also Rises* with a question—"Who is this W.H. Hudson?" After a few seconds of silence, he pressed again—"Doesn't *anyone* know?" I, out of twenty-five students, supplied the too enthusiastic, somewhat incoherent explanation that unfortunately put me in the same class as the estranged Cohn.

I have since discovered that there are other Hudson zealots, and they surface in the oddest places. When I began my research on Hudson for my doctoral thesis, the Cohns almost magically came out of hiding. One day while I was seated in a vegetarian restaurant thinking about those literary luncheons in the Mont Blanc, I was joined by an acquaintance who owned the most respected used book store in town. Unprompted, he told me that he had just finished reading "Tecla and the Little Men" and proceeded to deliver an informal lecture on an unknown poet—W.H. Hudson. Not much later, I was waiting in The Ear Inn in Soho, New York City when I began a conversation with a performance artist who rambled on and on about the friendship between Ford Madox Ford and W.H. Hudson.

During my dissertation years I came across a punk rock star whose favorite book is *Green Mansions*, the daughter of a rather staunch business man who was named after Rima, the bird-girl, and a technical writer who reads *Far Away and Long Ago* once a year.

Although his audience is select and varied, the Hudson readers have three things in common: they enjoy dreaming of, or temporarily believing in, impossibilities; they love the sound of language for its own sake; and they simply must know how others came to discover Hudson. When they meet someone who shares their penchant, they become animated, sometimes speechless. Eventually they ask their question—"How did *you* come across a writer who is never mentioned in a class room or displayed in book store windows?"

Hudson walked into my life by chance when I was taking an advanced literature course in high school. The teacher whose greatest talent was compiling bibliographies distributed a most organized list of suggestions for summer reading. When I was released for vacation I began to work my way down the alphabet until I came to "H." When I checked out *Green Mansions* I expected nothing less than a young governess, an old mansion (with gables, of course), a tea set, and possibly a ghost. What I didn't expect was to become so possessed by that book that I couldn't stop reading it for meals or for sleep, so enthralled that I would peruse it three more times, so converted that I forced every friend within a letter's radius to study it and discuss it with me, so excited that I began my hunt for other books on and by the same author, a quest which was not more fruitful than Abel's journey to Riolama. My local public library housed only three other books: *Far Away and Long Ago*, *The Purple Land*, and *A Little Boy Lost*.

My interest in Hudson did not wane with other childhood phases, but instead accompanied me to college where I composed an essay on Hudson for a writing course which the teacher read aloud to the class. My interest also survived graduate school where in four years of intense study of literature, Hudson's name only came up twice—once in connection with the infamous Cohn and once in the context of a lecture on Pound's unusual taste. Now that I think of it, it is a miracle that I found a doctoral committee willing to guide me through my many drafts of a book-length study of a writer about whom they knew little.

This book, a revision of the dissertation, is written for the individual who has at least read and appreciated *Green Mansions* and hopes to learn more about Hudson himself and his other books. My book introduces the author and focuses primarily on his later life in England. It has always puzzled me why biographies of Hudson favor those early years in Argentina when Hudson does it so beautifully himself in *Far Away and Long Ago* and when his real life, his life as a writer, began and ended in London. This book also attempts to show that he did not live in some mysterious vacuum: it describes the people he cared for and the characters he chose to include in his work. It also analyzes his adaptation of animism and Darwinism to his work as a naturalist. This book aims to provide a concise overview of the real Hudson and expose the remarkable variety within those twenty-four volumes of writing, a most substantial achievement. I also hope to reach the individual who has always felt some affinity with Cohn's romantic leanings.

List of Abbreviations

All page numbers from Hudson's books refer to the unnumbered volumes of *The Collected Works of W. H. Hudson* (New York: E. P. Dutton & Co., 1923) with the exception of *Green Mansions* which is the First American Edition, Revised with an Introduction by John Galsworthy (New York: Alfred A. Knopf, 1916). The abbreviations in chronological order are accompanied by the date of first publication. The last three refer to two volumes of letters and the biography. I have relied on the system of abbreviation suggested by Richard E. Haymaker in *From Pampas To Hedgerows and Downs* (New York: Bookman Associates, 1954).

PL	The Purple Land	1885
CA	A Crystal Age	1887
BLP	Birds of La Plata	1888-9
NLP	The Naturalist in La Plata	1892
FAN	Fan: The Story of a Young Girl's Life	1892
IDP	Idle Days in Patagonia	1893
BTV	Birds in Town and Village	1893
BL	Birds in London	1898
ND	Nature in Downland	1900
B&M	Birds and Man	1901
EO	El Ombú and Other South American Stories	1902
HD	Hampshire Days	1903
GM	Green Mansions	1904
LBL	A Little Boy Lost and Various Poems	1905
LE	The Land's End	1908
AIE	Afoot in England	1909

CHAPTER I

Hudson and His Contemporaries

WILLIAM HENRY HUDSON is interesting both as a man and as a writer. He had ties with three nations. Born in Argentina of New England parents, he lived in London for over forty-five years and actually became a British subject in 1900. Although the publication of *Green Mansions* in 1904 and the unveiling in Hyde Park of the controversial Rima Memorial sculpted by Jacob Epstein in 1925 expanded an always small readership, Hudson's loyal following consisted mainly of other writers who championed him as a great stylist.[1] Amongst these were Edward Garnett, Edward Thomas, Morley Roberts, John Galsworthy, Ford Madox Ford, Joseph Conrad, Violet Hunt, and Ezra Pound. Hudson considered himself a rebel against an age of divisiveness and therefore refused to restrict himself to a particular discipline. The complete works in twenty-four volumes, a mélange of fiction, poetry, autobiography, ornithology, out-of-door essays, and preservationist pamphlets for the Bird Society and Humanitarian League are unified by two common denominators: the worship of Nature as an ever-changing perfection and an expressed antipathy toward all forms of confinement.

1

Rima, the heroine of *Green Mansions*, personifies Nature
and appears so protean to Abel, her lover, that he finds himself
unable to assign a specific quality to her features: "The colour
of the skin would be almost impossible to describe, so greatly
did it vary with every change of mood—and the moods were
many and transient—and with the angle on which the sunlight
touched it, and the degree of light."[2] Since Rima agrees with
her surroundings, her hair color alters with the position of the
sun.

> In the shade, viewed closely, the general colour appeared a
> slate, deepening in places to purple but even in the shade the
> nimbus of free flossy hairs half veiled the darker tints with a
> downy pallor; and at a distance of a few yards it gave the
> whole hair a vague, misty appearance. In the sunlight the
> colour varied more, looking now dark, sometimes intensely
> black, now of a light uncertain hue, with a play of iridescent
> colour on the loose surface, as we see on the glossed plumage
> of some birds; and at a short distance, with the sun shining
> full on her head it sometimes looked white as a noonday
> cloud.[3]

Possibly Rima is a product of self-plagiarism. Yoletta, the heroine of *A Crystal Age*, Hudson's utopian novel published in
1887, seems to Smith, her admirer, to be a goddess of infinite
variety.

> Her eyes, at the distance I stood from her, appeared black or
> nearly black, but when seen closely they proved to be
> green—a wonderfully pure, tender sea green; . . . Her hair
> fell to her shoulders; but it was very wavy or curly, and
> strayed in small tendril-like tresses over her neck, forehead
> and cheeks; in color it was golden black—that is, black in
> shade, but when touched with sunlight every hair became a
> thread of shining red-gold; and in some lights it looked like
> raven-black hair powdered with gold-dust.[4]

Both protagonists, Abel and Smith, realize the futility of trying to find the one adjective which accurately captures this ever-shifting beauty. When faced with an impossible task, that of communicating infinitude itself, the characters discover that language becomes a hindrance rather than a vehicle.

Hudson also repeatedly expressed a dissatisfaction with words which he found both limiting and necessary. The nearly chimerical humming bird will not sit still for its portrait: "To give any true conception of it by means of mere word-painting is not more [possible] than it would be to bottle up a supply of the 'living sunbeams' themselves and convey them across the Atlantic to scatter them in a sparkling shower over the face of England."[5] The nonpasserine bird, like Rima, characterized by an unceasing motion and polychromatic surfaces, defies the singular and all too static adjective.

> The minute exquisite form when the bird hovers on misty wings, probing the flowers with its coral spear, the fan-like tail expanded and poising motionless, exhibits the feathers shot with many hues; and the next moment vanishes, or all but vanishes, then reappears at another flower only to vanish again, and soon successively, showing its splendours not continuously, but like the intermitted flashes of the firefly—this forms a picture of airy grace and loveliness that baffles description.[6]

Even in his nonfiction Hudson acknowledges the failure of language to reflect the ineffable radiance of all living things and the illusive soul of Nature.

Hudson's awareness of the imperfections of his medium also comes across in a style which at its best appears spontaneous, simple and lucid. It is a prose which has not only been over-praised, but too often compared with warblings and bubbling brooks: Herbert S. Gorman, the American biographer, novelist, and essayist, equates it with "the sweet notes of the robin" while Richard Aldington, poet and editor of *The Egoist*, turns to flowing water for his correlative:[7]

I felt as if I were sitting by a small stream of silvery water tumbling over brown mossy stones among green reeds on a sunny day, so that in one place the water seemed dark ochre, in another green, in another blue where the sky was reflected, and white where the water splashed over a little rock and gold when the sunlight touched the ripples. Only in this way can I express the feeling of fresh vivid colour and of harmonious language beautifully clear.[8]

Ford Madox Ford suggests that the rhythms and graphic descriptions are results of divine inspiration. He first quotes Conrad's response to *Green Mansions*: "You may try for ever to learn how Hudson got his effects and you will never know. He writes down his words as the good God makes the green grass to grow, and that is all you will ever find to say about it if you try for ever."[9] Ford then describes the detailed corrections on the rough drafts which he feels might produce that ostensibly artless quality.

He would substitute for the simple word *grew* the almost more simple word *were*. *When the hedges were green* for *when the hedges grew green*, not so much with the idea of avoiding alliteration as because there is an actual difference in the effect produced visually. You do not see that they are green. And I suppose these minute verbal alterations, meticulously attended to, did give his projected scenes their vividness.

Within a prose that fails in places, the passages that make his books worthwhile, usually those containing a word picture of some creature or outdoor setting, spring from a deep love of his subject and an intense frustration with language.

Hudson's struggle to compensate for the limitations imposed on him by words is only one manifestation of his protest against the even greater enemy, confinement itself. In his periodic escapes from the city he sought open spaces, the downs, the cliffs, the coastlines, which he liked to associate with his memories of the South American plains. Even the forest settings so often described in his books seemed at times too constraining. Also Hudson launched an attack on the practice of encaging wild creatures, especially the birds which to him stood for the very spirit of freedom. Hudson's claustrophobia expressed itself in even another way. He took great pains to avoid being categorized or labeled himself. Not only did he refuse to specialize, but he commingled his many fields within single books. This is not, as the poet Edward Thomas once pointed out, simply an effort to challenge the "supposed incompatibility of science with poetry."[10] Hudson did not perceive himself as a mere reconciler, but instead as a pioneer in a newly fledged form of expression which lies outside both the spheres of Art and Science.

Sometimes W.H. Hudson called himself a "field naturalist," which he defined in many different ways depending on his mood and purpose at the moment. The only definition which encompasses all levels of his work as a field naturalist is the one proferred at the close of *A Hind in Richmond Park* where Hudson takes the "whole wide world" for his scope.[11] Several of his contemporaries not only felt that Hudson attained his goal, but argued that because he incorporated everything in his books, he repelled many potential readers: H.J. Massingham, one who shared Hudson's interest in books and birds, explains why the nonconformity limited the audience:

> To the learned he was suspect because he mixed up natural history with religion, poetry, animism, fancy, emotion and the humanities. He would not fit in to the current definition of the arts because of his naturalism and his crusading spirit or into that of scientific analysis because such elements as vision and fantasy were considered irrelevant to it.[12]

John Galsworthy, who introduced Alfred A. Knopf, the publisher, to *Green Mansions* and composed a preface to this book, the revised American edition, and others, also believed that Hudson gained little recognition for his independence "in an age of specialism which loves to put men into pigeon-holes and label them."[13] Edward Garnett, the English critic, who worked to promote Hudson, argued that his books fall into that "peculiar class of independent and unconventional works of art which are destined to have but the scantiest audience for many years after their first appearance, for they neither ride on the wave of the tendency of their day nor do they carry within them the seed of any coming fashion."[14] Massingham, Galsworthy, and Garnett focus on results: they see Hudson as victor in a campaign against specialism and suggest that this greatness is precisely what limited his readership. I differ from their view in my emphasis on the goal, one which Hudson himself acknowledged as unattainable. I also do not believe that Hudson's select audience can be attributed to any one cause. However, I do feel that the goal itself, the dream of forging a new vocation without boundaries, brought about in his readers a variety of responses, all somewhat injurious to his reputation—mistrust, misunderstanding, irritation and hero-worship.

Hudson's war against confinement went even further than his refusal to fit himself into a set discipline. A larger, implicit goal underlies the complete works and sets Hudson apart from the countless number of other writers who have taken Nature as their topic. Hudson was not content to write *about* Nature; he wished to *be* Nature. Hudson tried to construct an image for himself which he felt would be compatible with the indefinability and variability of his topic. He wrote continually about fusing with his environment: "If a man be capable of an exalted mood, of a sense of absolute freedom, so that he is no longer flesh and spirit but both in one, and one with nature, it comes to him like some miraculous gift on a hill or down or wide open heath."[15] Hudson believed that the man who experiences this true bond with the everchanging expanse of Nature is also impossible to pin down. Hudson worked to present himself as free, illusive and protean. In later life he wished to exert complete control over his self image; he periodically burned letters and personal documents and tried to influence potential critics and biographers.

Morley Roberts, novelist and critic, published *A Portrait* in 1924 which was not intended to be a factual biography, but a character study and an account of a friendship. The book borders on pure panegyric. Not only does Roberts perceive Hudson's idiosyncrasies as evidence of heroism, but dignifies the naturalist's lifelong efforts to be known as the inscrutable enigma. This is how Roberts opens the book:

> To reach any vision whatever of a human being who even then baffled eyes which had seen him grow into full manhood is not a task for the intellect, but if it comes at all, a gift to long-lasting affection and comradeship. To reckon up Hudson in intellectual terms would be a vain task. To build him from his books, self-revealing as they may be, would give much but leave more unsaid. There was something in his character which forbade him to abandon his soul to others. He kept it in a strong secret place, as those fabled giants in ancient myths keep theirs.[16]

The word "myth" which surfaces on the first page of *A Portrait* is important for two reasons: it is central to the work of W.H. Hudson, the animist, who not only anthropomorphized Nature, but also mythologized himself. It also pertains to the Hudson devotees who helped to put forth a fictionalized image, create a mysterious hero.

This aggrandizement of W.H. Hudson seems most pronounced in *A Portrait*, the most complete study by a contemporary. Occasionally Roberts portrays his bird-man as a nature deity: "At times he seemed some ancient Pan who loved the withering leaves in ancient woods of autumn (he loved to move in the fallen beech leaves of late October or November), and as he sat and watched the birds one wondered why they did not come to him as the wild creatures of the Galapagos came to

his congener Darwin."[17] Other times, Roberts refuses to allow
his subject any imperfections and defends him against many
nameless attacks:

> Those who do not see his greatness, though it may defy
> analysis, are not to be envied. What, indeed is a great man? Is
> the word to be confined to conquerors? Hudson conquered
> the English tongue and made of it an instrument of rarest
> music. Or to artists? What else was he but an artist whose
> pictures of the wildest or most homely English life convey
> more than any painting, and are themselves poems? To those
> who alter the destinies of men as philosophers and politi-
> cians? Then he has altered the whole outlook of thousands
> and taught them mercy, pity, love and beautiful words.
> There is, too, a greatness in character alone.[18]

Despite Roberts's glorification of Hudson, *A Portrait* is
certainly not useless: it contains some recorded conversations
and straight-forward anecdotes which disclose Hudson's more
human side—his hypochondria, his frequent irritability.

Morley Roberts is not the only writer to suggest that
Hudson defied analysis. Ford Madox Ford claims to be so awed
by this inscrutable God that he admits to experiencing a kind of
verbal apoplexy not unlike that of Abel straining to find words
to describe Rima's tresses:

> For a long, long time, I daresay for twenty-five years—I have
> been longing to say something about Mr. Hudson. But what
> is there to say? Of things immense, tranquil or consummate,
> it is difficult to speak or to write. The words are at the tip of
> the tongue: the ideas at the back of the brain . . . and yet:
> Nothing! So one says, 'immense,' 'tranquil,' 'con-
> summate.'[19]

Then Ford lunges into a paean, one which exemplifies the
animation and excessive zeal expressed in so many portraits,
reviews, and appreciations of W.H. Hudson.

Suppose one should say that one would willingly cancel every one of the forty or so books that one has published if one could be given the power to write one paragraph as this great poet writes a paragraph or that one would willingly give up all one's powers of visualising this and that if one could be granted this great naturalist's power of looking at a little bird . . . One might say—and indeed I do say with perfect sincerity—that one would willingly sacrifice all one's gifts as a master of English ten years longer of writing life. . . . But even that would be selfish—for one would have the pleasure: one would read what he wrote.[20]

Ford extends this reverence for the writer to the man who seemed to him nearly omniscient: "You walked beside him, he stalking along and, from far above you, Olympianly destroying your theories with accurate dogma."[21] He recalls his weekly luncheons at the Mont Blanc with Hudson as the nucleus of the group. He remembers the entrance of the legendary South American that left the others, the mortal writers,"breathless."[22] Ford, like Roberts, believed that "there was no one—no writer—who did not acknowledge without question that this composed giant was the greatest living writer of English."[23] The Hudson portrayed in these articles appears larger than life and as inexplicable as Nature.

Violet Hunt's retrospections resemble Ford's in tone and in her magnification of Hudson into the deific prophet. In *The English Review* she writes about inviting "a young literary aspirant" to tea "to meet the most charming man in the world" whom she calls "Huddie," has known since childhood, and claims is "the most beautiful human being [her] eyes have ever rested upon."[24] She foreshadows the real incident of the article by explaining that "even she did not realise that Beauty must fade so soon," and then moves toward the funeral, attended by Morley Roberts, the most demonstrative mourner, an event which struck her as understated and anticlimactic.

No one cried but Mr. R., who, after throwing his sprigs of

heather down, walked away, stumbling over the graves. The vicar departed, and the local reporters pattered about, scrutinising names on the wreaths and asking questions of anyone who would answer. Some of the mourners, informed that the grave of Richard Jefferies was only five minutes' walk, went to look at it.[25]

She expresses her reluctance to leave him alone in the grave "withouten any company," reflects upon funerals and that "cold ditch six feet long by three feet wide" as components to what Hudson himself termed "the Monstrous Betrayal." After scolding "ruthless" and "utilitarian" humanity and burials, she resolves to "return home, and, reading again with reverence *The Return of the Chiff-Chaff*, learn from him the submission he practiced and preached." Violet Hunt speaks of W. H. Hudson as a religion and his writings as the holy writ.

R. B. Cunninghame Graham also perceives his close friend as the seer and as a source of revelation. Shortly before his own death, Graham made a pilgrimage to Hudson's birthplace, the "House of the Twenty-Five Ombú Trees" near Buenos Aires. Dr. Fernando Pozzo, whom Graham calls "the greatest lover and prophet of Hudson in the New World," who was then working on a translation of *Far Away and Long Ago*, accompanied him on the journey and recorded it in the *Nación* of Buenos Aires.[26] Both this translated article and Graham's letters to Roberts and Garnett printed in *The Living Age* reveal a religious veneration for Hudson's boyhood home and the surrounding terrain. In the letter Graham "dictated with great feeling and with tears in his eyes," he explains to Roberts that although he has travelled widely "to Rome, to Santiago de Compostella and other places well known to the whole world" he has "never been more impressed at any of these places than [he is] in this humble *rancho* with its wooden roof, its brick floors, its primitive doors and its air of aloofness from everything modern (*gracias a Dios*)." Graham lists the details which have altered mimimally since Hudson's youth as he addresses a fellow worshiper:

> All the plants that Hudson loved, fennel, evening primrose and the rest are here to mourn him. . . . There is a chestnut horse, unfortunately a *mestizo*, tied to a post in front of the house. It is, I think, waiting for Hudson to throw a sheepskin on its back and ride down to the *arroyo* to water it. You will understand in the way that the villagers in Cornwall understood when they cut upon the stone 'W. H. Hudson used to sit here.'

Right up until his final moment Graham worked on translating Hudson into Spanish.[27] From his death-bed he describes to Edward Garnett the experience of "writing in that little room and thinking that from such unlikely surroundings so great a genius had arisen."[28] Graham also pleads with his countrymen to erect a memorial for "a great Englishman whose Nature writings are inspired by that change of heart towards wild life which is replacing the old indifference and spirit of destruction."[29] Graham who himself lived in Argentina idolizes Hudson as the inimitable Nature writer.

Even Ezra Pound who does not applaud easily perpetuates in his letters and in *The Little Review* the image of Hudson as a mysterious demigod. He sees in the books a perfect combination of "enthusiasm for his subject matter," heightened sensitivity and acute perception.[30] He says, "Hudson is an excellent example of Coleridge's theorem 'the miracle that can be wrought' simply by one man's feeling something more keenly, or knowing it more intimately than it has been, before, known." Pound refers to the power of "quiet charm" which allures even him through books with seemingly inane titles into worlds which normally wouldn't entice him.[31]

He would lead us to South America; despite the gnats and

mosquitoes we would all perform the voyage for the sake of meeting a puma, Chimbića, friend of man, the most loyal of wildcats. And as I am writing this presumably for an audience, more or less familiar with my predilections, familiar with my loathing of sheep, my continual search for signs of intelligence in the human race, it should be some indication of Hudson's style that it has carried even me through a volume entitled 'A Shepherd's Life,' a title which has no metaphorical bearing, but deals literally with the subject indicated.

Indeed it is challenging to imagine Ezra Pound engaged in the lives of the Bawcombe shepherds, watching two ravens in combat, following the tale of a fox-hunting sheepdog, or even tolerating Hudson's ongoing quarrel with formal education and book learning. But Pound explains that only this great stylist can make him fall "completely under the spell of a chapter with no more startling subject matter than the cat at a rural station of an undistinguished British provincial railway."[32] Midway through his article, Pound finds himself with an "arranging of hierarchies and an awarding of medals for merit."[33] He places Hudson's scenery on the top with Hardy's countrysides and alongside "Hueffer when dealing with La Plata." Pound finally ranks Hudson's prose superior to that of Edgar Allan Poe which is "an art of a very high order."[34]

These endorsements of W. H. Hudson do not stand alone. Sorting through essays, reviews, portraits and reminiscences leads to a discovery of many unsupported and often excessive eulogies. The mythological Hudson comes across as the enigma, the Olympian, the prophet, the genius, and the deific stylist. In fact, in *W. H. Hudson: Bird-Man*, an early book-length study, Harold Goddard, then head of the English Department at Swarthmore College, goes so far as to suggest that Hudson equals ideal humanity and sees "man, *homo sapiens*, evolving in the direction of bird-man, homo Hudsonius."[35] I believe this trend of hero-worship in the literature springs both from the desire on the part of readers to promote what they felt was a neglected author and from the image Hudson constructed for himself, the embodiment of everchanging Nature which cannot be confined by a field, a description, a label, a single word. This self-presentation which comes across not in any one passage, but in the collected works as a whole is indeed seductive: when reading Hudson it is always difficult to distinguish between his impossible aspirations and his actual achievements.

CHAPTER II

A New Life In England

WILLIAM HENRY HUDSON, age thirty-three, sailing from Argentina to England on board the *Ebro* on April 1, 1874, saw himself as embarking on a new chapter in his life. Many factors played a part in Hudson's decision to migrate. The loss of family ties and lack of career opportunity caused Hudson to let go of his hold on *Los Veinte-Cinco Ombúes* where only his youngest sister remained. It also seems likely that his chronic heart condition led him to seek more sophisticated medical assistance in London. But most significant were Hudson's previously established ties in the field of natural history which made a career in London look promising. In 1868 Dr. P. L. Sclater, a London ornithologist to whom Hudson's collections had been sent, wrote to inform the young birdman that his name would be included in the *Proceedings* of the Zoological Society. When his first published work on Argentine birds appeared on December 14, 1869, in the form of a letter, Hudson began to consider the possibilities of gaining a wider circulation in England. In addition to this promising correspondence, it may be assumed that the joint project, *Argentine Ornithology*, which appeared in 1888–9, Sclater supplying the scientific data and Hudson the field notes and observations, had been planned before Hudson left his country.[1] On the *Ebro* Hudson felt he was moving toward new hope, new opportunities.

After Hudson arrived in England, he spent a few days at Southampton, visited the Isle of Wight and then stayed a short time with the family of a South American friend who was living at Malmesbury. In his diary when he describes his early explorations, he expresses an infatuation with his new home: he calls Southampton "a beautiful place" with "wide clean macadam streets, grand old elm and horse-chestnut trees—parks covered with velvety turf—gothic churches and ancient stone buildings covered to their summits with ivy."[2] Right from the start he establishes his pattern of comparing England to Argentina and says, "Altogether day in England is like the hurried, misty, dreamy fresh morning twilight of Buenos Ayres." Hudson's account of his first countryside ramble in England reveals his delight in discovery that would become characteristic of his later collections of out-of-door essays.

> Yesterday I walked several miles out into the country and found it looked just as I imagined it would. I went along a beautiful carriage drive which runs to Winchester, but didn't keep to the road: on either side were clumps and groves of magnificient trees, elm, oak, spruce, pine, etc., the grass was like velvet and spread with little flowers. One I knew was the 'wee modest crimson tippet flower,' I also knew the 'wild violet' and one I took for the butter cup.[3]

Once in England Hudson couldn't wait to begin his bird watching; he writes his brother about the thrushes and the cuckoo "warbling his mysterious lay from grove to grove." The diary ends prematurely on May 9, 1874 before he could relay his intial reactions to London. Hudson explains that the diary is becoming too voluminous, that if he "writes on this scale [his] London letter will fill three volumes."[4] No record of these first impressions of the big city has been discovered.

15

Shortly after his arrival in London, Hudson began work on *Argentine Ornithology* and received little payment. He also tried his hand at writing short articles, but these unsuccesful beginnings have not survived. Two major disappointments added to this discouragement: he paid a visit to John Gould, one of his idols, an ornithologist known for his studies of hummingbirds, and there he met the ill-tempered scientist who returned his admiration with mockery and rejection. Later he was engaged as a secretary to a bankrupt archaeologist, Chester Waters, who constructed genealogies for Americans. Morley Roberts describes the fiasco that Hudson once told to him.

This man employed Hudson to look up pedigrees and the like, not that he could afford a secretary, but because he was unable to leave his house, as he was besieged by creditors and catchpolls. At times food was introduced by means of cords lowered from upper windows, and often Hudson could not get into the house because he would have been followed by bailiffs. It was sometimes as difficult for him to leave it. As may be imagined, his salary was always in arrears and he and his employer had periodical combats about money. Waters used to say, 'It is no use asking me for money. I haven't any.'[5]

After approximately three years of struggling to make a living, Hudson met and married Emily Wingrave, a singer and boarding-house keeper in Leinster Square, Bayswater. For many years the two of them endured poverty together: Hudson once confessed that he and Emily lived for an entire week on a tin of cocoa and milk.[6]

In 1879 Morley Roberts walked into this house at Leinster Square and met the man who was to exert the most powerful influence over his life and writing.[7] Right from the inception of the friendship, Roberts perceived a man of "great stature" who "carried the breath of the pampa with him."[8] Roberts repeatedly equates Hudson's life with his wife who was fifteen to twenty years his senior to the cruel imprisonment of a wild and untamed spirit: "To think of Hudson merely *in* a boarding-house seems an absurdity, nay, even a cruelty, as it is to pen eagles in cages; but to contemplate him, if not as the keeper of such a place, as the husband of one who was seems beyond all words."[9] Apparently the Hudson's move in 1886 to a house on St. Luke's Road in Westbourne Park, London, inherited by Emily, where Hudson lived for the rest of his life, brought him no relief, no major improvements. Although Tower House, as it was called, was by no means ideal for a nature-lover, it was not the real cause of Hudson's dark years. It was Hudson's frustrated efforts to make it in the literary world that brought about the feeling of entrapment. At first, Hudson simply could not break into the market. The first of his articles to be published, "Wanted—A Lullaby," by "Maud Merryweather" appeared in Cassell's *Family Magazine* in March 1875. Hudson speaks as a mother lamenting the fact that there is no national lullaby to compare with Spanish cradle songs. Beyond that first well-written, but trivial essay, *The Purple Land*, his first massive achievement, originally entitled *The History of the House of Lamb*, an adventure set in the Banda Oriental, did not appear until eleven years after his arrival in England. Hudson's early novella, *Ralph Herne*, the tale of a young doctor during the yellow fever epidemic in Buenos Aires, was not accepted until 1888 when the editor of *Youth* agreed to print it as a serial.

Hudson never let go of his memories of these penniless days when manuscript after manuscript was rejected. Even in 1903 when the tables had turned, when publishers were begging him for articles, he still harbored some resentment: "What revolts me is the thought that when I had not a penny and almost went down on my knees to editors, publishers and literary agents I couldn't even get a civil word, and of ten—or perhaps twenty—MSS. sent, nine (or nineteen) would be sent back."[10] Hudson does not limit his attacks on the journalistic world to his private letters, but this rage frequently obtrudes from the otherwise calm and steady flow of his narrative voice in fiction.

This blatantly occurs in *Fan* , the story of a young girl's rise in social class, a novel published under the pseudonym of Henry Hartford in 1892. Hudson is describing Merton's efforts to quash his wife's hopes to make a living as a writer in the world of predatorial editors.

> He concluded with a comical description of the magazine editor as a very unhappy spider, against whose huge geometric web there beats a continuous rain of dipterous insects of every known variety, besides innumerable nondescripts. The poor spider, unable to eat and digest more than about half a dozen to a dozen flies every month, was forced to spend the whole time cutting and dropping his useless captures from the Web.[11]

Here Merton, a weak hypocrite who "would not tell the truth if a lie could serve his purpose equally well," turns into an araneidan naturalist and articulates Hudson's own gripes.[12]

By the turn of the century the quality of Hudson's life had improved considerably. In 1901 Lord Grey, the liberal statesman and naturalist, granted him an annual civil list pension of 150 pounds. In addition, the Knopf publication of *Green Mansions*, published in 1916, sold beautifully in America. In his letters to Morley Roberts, Hudson sounds bewildered by his own sudden popularity. In 1916 he describes publishers fighting for possession of his books and with his characteristic touch of bitterness reminds Roberts that this was not always the case.

> I hear from America that two publishers are quarrelling over my books. Dutton who never did and never would do anything with them and said they were too English, not 'sweet' enough for American readers, now pretends that he has always been enthusiastic about them and is bringing out new editions of *A Crystal Age* and *The Purple Land*, with forewords by Roosevelt. . . . It would amuse me very much if the sudden popularity had not come so late in the day.[13]

When Hudson's finances became so sound because of *Green Mansions'* sizeable profits, Hudson voluntarily relinquished his pension. His financial well-being was accompanied by a noticeable change in his attitude toward his adopted country: England became his cause, his philosophy and his work.

Hudson's life in London provided him with the material to continue his fight against the ills of city life, the fumes, decay, and toxins, the qualities that seemed most oppressive during his more difficult years. In a letter written in 1902, he speaks of the city as a bane: "I fancy London is poisonous and poisons a man most when he has been out of it for some time, breathing air not laden with carbonic acid gas, and eating food not kept from decaying by means of formalin, boracic acid and salicylates."[14] But Hudson did not blame England alone for the misery he saw in city life. Rather, London replaced Buenos Aires as his target in his campaign against the evils of urbanization which he saw spreading indiscriminately across the globe.

In *Far Away and Long Ago* Argentina's main city is the villain which "practically brought the happy time of [his] boyhood to an end."[15] He fixes on the abomination, Saladero, the killing-grounds for cattle, horses, and sheep, and describes the "wild shouts of the slaughterers and the awful bellowings of the tortured beasts."[16] He defines Buenos Aires as the "city of evil smells . . . the chief pestilential city of the globe" that had to "call in engineers from England to do something to save the inhabitants from extinction."[17] Young Hudson also fell prey to the poor sanitation and living conditions, and after a period of perplexing lassitude and depression, he wound up with "the dread typhus, an almost obsolete malady in Europe."[18] Not long after a miraculous recovery, Hudson, still in a weakened condition, exposed himself to the elements and developed rheumatic fever which left him with a permanently damaged heart. In later years Hudson blamed his debilities on that visit to Buenos Aires and expanded this into a campaign against urbanization.

19

In *Ralph Herne*, probably written before Hudson ever left South America, he exploits the horror of the yellow-fever epidemic to persuade his readers that the city itself is the real infection. This early novella with its artificial characters and often ludicrous dialogue gets its entire substance from those chapters that describe the city's inability to cope with its self-induced destruction:

> People dropped down, writhed for a few hours in unspeakable agonies, then died, and no power could save them from dying. Such a condition of things had perhaps never been known, for it seemed that no pestilence comparable in deadly virulence to this had ever fallen on any city ancient and modern. Men were seen rushing about the streets apparently insane with terror. The municipality exhusted all its futile measures of prevention, using disinfectants to such an extent that the atmosphere became stifling with the smells of carbolic acid and chloride of lime; while the slightest breeze blew up a cloud of minute, white, lime-dust particles that blinded the eyes and choked the lungs.[19]

Not surprisingly these pictures of Buenos Aires battling its plague do not differ greatly from Hudson's later accounts of scenes in everyday London. In the later works London exemplified the inhumane conditions, the state in opposition to nature.

In "The London Sparrow," an essay in blank verse first printed in *Merry England* in 1883, the narrator, who feels exiled from the avian race, haunted by scenes of a childhood spent in a distant land with marshes and woods, commiserates with the sparrow doomed to a dreary existence in London.[20] The prisoner questions why the sparrow, endowed by Nature with a means to escape, settles for incarceration; he goes on to express Hudson's own conviction that city life begrimes the spirit and deprives us of our true intended identity:

Imprisoned in a lurid atmosphere

That maketh all things black and desolate,
Until, as in a coin illegible
To keenest Antiquary, lost are all
The signs that mark thy kind—the pretty gloss
That Nature gave thee clouded and confounded,
Till to the ornithologist thou art
A bird ambiguous, to others, too
A thing offensive.

The speaker describes his view of London, a possible rendition of the scene from Hudson's boarding-house window:

a desert desolate
Of fabrics gaunt and grim and smoke-begrimed,
By goblin misery haunted, scowling towers
Of cloud and stone, gigantic tenements
And castles of despair . . .

For the exile, the sparrow represents a "living link" to his native land, a creature that "binds [him] to the immemorial past," that provides him with some consolation in his blackened cell. Finally Hudson's sparrow evolves into a symbol of the timeless spirit of Nature which is independent of perishable humanity that constructs transitory worlds.

So, gleaner unregarded, flittest thou—
Now, as of old, and in years to come,
Nature's one witness, till the murmuring sound
Of human feet unnunbered, like the rain
Of summer pattering on the forest leaves,
Fainter and fainter falling 'midst the ruin,
In everlasting silence dies away.

Hudson saw the metropolis as a wasteland and often contrasted it with bird life suggestive of immortality and indestructible freedom.

Hudson's prose exposé of the evils of London occurs in *Fan*, the story of a girl who is bred in the slums with a drunken mother and brutal foster father and who, through the friendship of a lady, rises in social class. Although the plot is incredible and too sentimental, the pictures of London are realistic and forceful. Hudson begins the novel with a description of the crude tenement and of Fan's mother who is "almost repulsive to look at . . . in her dirty, ill-fitting gown, with her feet thrust out before her, showing her broken muddy boots."[21] When her husband threatens her with violence, Fan is sent out into the "rough brutish world of the London streets" to beg for the coppers that will appease his temper.[22] In the first part of the novel Hudson sums up the life of the destitute in London and attempts to reveal every genus and species within the street masses—the auctioneers, quacks, minstrels, jugglers, and costermongers. Hudson forces the reader to peer through those "clouded windowpanes" of the public bars, and through Fan's surprising innocence, to share his vision of the homeless waifs which he describes with as much precision as the specimens in his books on ornithology.[23] The following passage, a portrait of one city victim, typifies the kind of critique of London life found in the earlier part of the novel.

> At one spot her attention was painfully held by a short, dark, misshapen man with no hands nor arms but only the stump of an arm with a stick tied to it. Before him on a rough stand was a board, with half a dozen thick metal wires stretched across it. Rapidly moving his one poor stump he struck on the wires with his stick and so produced a succession of sounds that roughly resembled a tune. Poor man, how she pitied him.

In Fan's London, human beings are reduced to savages and machines. Later on, Fan watches her mother murdered in a brawl with a drunken rival. The two combatants beat each other with an "insane fury" while spectators, depicted as a composite beast, egg them on.[24] The street fight turns into a scathing commentary on the mutant *Homo Sapien* grazing on the poisons of the metropolis. Hudson probes the psychology behind the women tearing each other apart and behind the city dwellers lusting for entertainment.

> Not one in the throng remembered that he had an old mother, a pale-faced wife and little children at home, and sisters, working-girls perhaps. For the working man has a sporting instinct as well as his betters; he cannot gratify it by seeing stripped athletic men pounding each other with their fists at Pelican clubs; he has only the occasional street fight to delight his soul, and the spectacle of two maddened women tearing each other is not one to be ungrateful for.

Once Fan's mother is knocked unconscious, this affects a catharsis. The crowd, as diabolical as the aborigines who burn the daughter of Didi, disperses. For a time Fan drifts through impoverished communities, herself orphaned and starving. Later Hudson suggests that the ills of modern life go much deeper than poverty. Fan, although rescued by Mary Starbow, and freed from worring about necessities, finds herself initiated into the more complex problems of the civilized world—selfishness, deceit, jealousy, betrayal—all bacteria cultured on the agar of urbanization.

The question naturally arises: why when a man disliked the city so much did he choose to remain there? Why did Hudson, even after his finances improved, cling to his life in Tower House and suffer that long climb to the garret floor with his impaired heart? As time passed Hudson felt rooted to the city because of his work; he saw London as the radius of his literary activities and found Tower House to be both a convenient work space and symbol of stability. Throughout his life in London, he kept alive his nomadic spirit: he and his wife took long walks and travelled through the countryside. In *Afoot in England* Hudson explains that these journeys were their sole source of pleasure and recreation during their more difficult years:

It occasionally happened that an article sent to some other magazine was not returned, and always after so many rejections to have one accepted and paid for with a cheque worth several pounds was a cause of astonishment, and was truly a miracle as if the angel of the sun had compassionately thrown us down a handful of gold. And out of these handfuls enough was sometimes saved for the country rambles at Easter and Whitsuntide and in the autumn.[25]

For Hudson, these excursions became a personal form of rebellion against the city.

That greater place we have been in, that mighty monstrous London, is ever present to the mind and is like a mist before the sight when we look at other places: but for me there is no such mist, no image so immense and persistent as to cover and obscure all others, and no such mental habit as that of regarding people as a mere crowd, a mass, a monstrous organism, in and on which each individual's but a cell, a scale. This feeling troubles and confuses my mind when I am in London where we live 'too thick' but quitting it I am absolutely free; it has not entered my soul and coloured me with its colour or shut me out from those who have never known it, even of the simplest dwellers on the soil who, to our sophisticated minds, may seem like beings of another species. This is my happiness—to feel, in all places that I am one with them.[26]

Not only does he express the wish to escape the thickness of London, but also determines to discard the depersonalization associated with the city. The excursion becomes therapeutic: once free from the mist, the distortion, Hudson can fix on the individual and the magic of ordinary life—the gleam in an eye, women carrying baskets, a gypsy with a cart, the lines on a floral petal, a shepherd with his dog, an old woman in the graveyard. In his countryside essays Hudson renders the frequently unnoticed details of rural life.

In letters Hudson often communicated to Morley Roberts

that London failed to satisfy his yen for boundlessness: in 1906, "I like open worlds—downs or great moors like the Cornish or Yorkshire ones;"[27] in 1907, from Land's End, he speaks of a favorite pastime: "of late I've lived pretty much out of doors, rambling on the cliffs and on the moors, listening to the chiff-chaff, or any feathered creatures we get here and in friendly talk with the natives."[28] These declarations of love for the downs, cliffs, moors, and coastlines are born out in each of his five collections of essays: *Nature in Downland, Hampshire Days, The Land's End, Afoot in England,* and *A Shepherd's Life.* Throughout these volumes Hudson always includes the "I" as the integral character against the larger background. The speaker in *Nature in Downland* puts the scene before us as he weaves in his own reactions to "the grey glinting ocean" and the "chalk cliffs"; he shows us "the living garment of the downs, its animal and vegetable forms, from the point of view of the lover of nature and, in a moderate degree, of the field naturalist."[29] It is characteristic of these books that throughout the catalogue of creatures, landscape, and peasants, we never lose track of the naturalist himself. The books are not just descriptions of out-of-the-way places in England, but instead accounts of Hudson's ever evolving relationship with his new country.

In *Hampshire Days* Hudson explains that he never feels estranged from the inhabitants of any rural village or wilderness area. His visit to the "Pixie mounds, the barrows raised by probably prehistoric men, a people inconceivably remote in time and spirit from us, whose memory is pale in our civilised days" propels him into a definition of "world-strangeness" and an assertion of his anti-town position.[30]

> I feel the 'strangeness' only with regard to my fellow men especially in towns, where they exist in conditions unnatural to me, but congenial to them; where they are seen in numbers and in crowds, in streets and houses, and in all places where they gather together; when I look on them, their pale civilised faces, their clothes, and hear them eagerly talking

about things that do not concern me. They are out of my
world—the real world.

Hudson distinguishes between his "real world" and the unnatural existence, the false ideas which are "nothing but by-
products, or growths of the artificial life—little funguses cultivated in heated cellars." When Hudson closes *Hampshire Days*
with a natural concerto, the music at dusk in a primordial kingdom, he also indirectly composes a song of protest against the
din of factories, the cranking of machines.

In *Afoot in England*, a miscellany of impressions of Salisbury, Bath, Wells, Stonehenge, Silchester and Whitesheet
Hill, Hudson assumes the persona of the spontaneous itinerant
who sets out to explore remote regions divested of all the trap-
pings of civilization—guidebooks, maps, and plans. The book
not only includes many passages about the cultivated art of
wandering, but discloses Hudson's characteristic restlessness.
On his quest for the "illusive, mysterious and inexpressibly
beautiful," he reaches "South Devon, the greenest, most
luxuriant in its vegetation and perhaps the hottest in
England."[31] Hudson finds that this land he at first perceived as
a new Eden, "loses its attraction over time." He begins to feel
trapped by the vegetation and starts dreaming of mountains or
plains "where there would be a wide horizon and wind blowing
unobstructed over leagues of open country to bring [him] back
the sense of lost liberty."[32] Any journey not radically different
from the confinement of London was often abandoned.

In *A Shepherd's Life* Hudson limits his focus to one
specific region, the Wiltshire Downs, and fixes primarily on
one man, a fictitious Caleb Bawcombe of a fictitious Winterbourne Bishop. Apparently Hudson spent some time with
James Lawes in Martin and wished to reproduce his anecdotes,
life story, and in the process describe the impressive surroundings. Consistently Hudson dispraises the results of moderni-
zation and mourns the passing away of methods of farming and

shepherding in England. In his quest for the unchanged, Hudson comes upon Winterbourne Bishop where if a man returned to life after a long sleep, he would see few alterations:

> He would see no mansion or big building, no puff of white steam and sight of a long black train creeping over the earth, nor any other strange thing. It would appear to him even as he knew it before he fell asleep—the same familiar scene, with furze and bramble and bracken on the slope, the wide expanse with sheep and cattle grazing in the distance, and the dark green of trees in the hollows and fold on fold of the low down beyond, stretching away to the dim, farthest horizon.[33]

This tribute to Winterbourne Bishop had such a strong impact on his readers that many were moved to seek out its true identity and experience this retreat for themselves. Even after Morley Roberts complained that he could not find the renamed village on any map, Hudson refused to rescind his vows of secrecy.[34]

Infrequently Hudson made a direct plea to his reader to preserve the land from commercial exploitation. Such an argument comprises the coda in *The Land's End*, an account of Hudson's experiences in Cornwall. The most stirring section of an otherwise uneven book begins with Hudson's discussion of the influx of pilgrims from all over England to Land's End. Hudson studies the men seated on the rocks and detects a common spirit there, a weariness and otherworldliness: they sit "silently gazing in one direction beyond that rocky foreland, with the same look of infinite weariness on their gray faces and in their dim sad eyes, as if one thought and feeling and motive had drawn them to this spot."[35] Land's End becomes a refuge for this aging pilgrim who sits "dreaming little and thinking less, while year by year and age by age the memory of the world of passion and of striving of which he was so unutterably tired grows fainter and fainter in his mind."[36] After Hudson brings out the sacred charm of the place, he introduces the mutilating forces of progress, "the men so devoid of sentiment and imagination that they would not hesitate to stamp out the last beautiful thing on earth, if its beauty, or some sentiment connected with it which made it seem beautiful is the only reason or the only excuse that can be given for its existence."[37] After appealing to the emotions, Hudson closes with a formal proposal to save the headland. He encourages the formation of a Cornish Society dedicated to the preservation of the land and the raising of funds by public subscription. This argument expresses his belief that Nature can and will survive the encroachment of progress and reveals an active involvement in preserving the natural beauty of his adopted country.

While in London, Hudson devoted his energy to the preservation of birds and the protection of wild life, an activity which controlled his decisions and convictions. The Society for the Protection of Birds, formed in Manchester in 1887, originally consisted of women pledged to avoid feathered decorations on their clothing and hats, a style much in vogue at the time. Hudson regularly attended these "Fur, Fin and Feather" gatherings at the home of Mrs. Edward Phillips who was to become the Vice President of the society. In 1891 a group of pamphlets appeared which Hudson wrote for the new society whose headquarters had shifted to London. *Osprey: or Egrets and Aigrettes* and *Save the Herons* were followed by a continuous stream of tracts issued by the Humanitarian League and Bird Society or written to some newspaper in the form of a letter of protest. Amongst these are such titles as *Bird-Catching, On Liberating Caged Birds, A Thrush that Never Lived, Letter to Clergymen, Ministers, and Others, Feathered Women* and *The Trade in Bird's Feathers*. In these writings there are essentially two voices at work; the informative and the invective. Hudson either tries to encourage people to protect the wild life by calmly supplying them with facts and descriptions or he attempts to alarm readers by bitterly lashing out at the violators of nature.

In *Adventures Among Birds* Hudson divides his enemies into three factions: first, "the barbarians of means who are devoted mainly to sport, and would cheerfully see the destruction of most of our birds above the size of a thrush for the sake of that disastrous exotic, the semi-domestic pheasant of the preserves; secondly, the private collector, that 'curse of rural England'; and last but not least, the regiment of horrible women who persist in decorating their heads with aigrettes and carcasses of slaughtered birds."[38] To add to this list of villains there are the bird-jailers Hudson fiercely condemns in *Nature in Downland*. Hudson's indictment of Chichester, the most filthy, morally diseased community encountered on his travels through England becomes his introduction to three pathetic prisoners: the jackdaw and black bird "were kept in rabbit-hutch-like cages fixed against the ceiling of a long, narrow, dimly-lighted passage."[39] The third victim, an owl, "even worse off than the others," barely existed "in an always malodorous and usually uncovered cage, in the kitchen, where a big fire was burning sixteen to seventeen hours every day." First, Hudson comments on the misery of the jackdaw:

> He made no cry, and had no hope of ever feeling the wind and the sun, or ever seeing the blue sky and green earth again. Eight to nine years had he been immured in that cursed prison, and he would never leave it until his tortured life had left him; then his dead body would be taken out, and another bird, I daresay, put there in his place.

This description resembles Hudson's exposé of the warped mind of the bird-jailer in the Preface to *The Other Side of the Bars*, a pamphlet published by Ernest Bell in 1911 explicitly for the Humanitarian League.

> Here is a being made to exist joyously under the sky, in sun and wind and rain; to inhabit the air by means of its marvellous structure and faculty of flight—come let's capture and

29

bring it into close interiors out of the sun and wind, and shut it in a cage so that it may never fly again![40]

But the argument in *Nature in Downland* had more power because of the speaker's own involvement with the captives. He arouses sympathy for the owl he befriends, a creature treated as a replaceable knick knack.

> The heat must have been—and alas! still must be—dreadful to the poor bird; but if speech had been given him he would, I think, have complained most of the gas jets: they were burning all about him until twelve o'clock every night, and the sensation they produced must have been as of fine heated needles, heated red and heated white, stabbing and pricking his sensitive eye-balls. In this chamber of torture the miserable bird had existed for nine months.

The sight of such agony moves Hudson toward delicate diplomacy. He approaches the landlady to plead the owl's case, prepares her for his request with flattery, praising her "greatly for her merciful heart" and informing her of "her fame in Chichester as a lover and protector of animals." At first, victory comes easily and she is persuaded to let him set the creature free. After he exhausts much time and energy finding the suitable home for it in the barn of a nearby farmhouse, the crone changes her mind. Although Hudson "begged and pleaded, not that day only, but the next and for several days," the landlady "would not part with the bird for love or money."[41] Hudson sees his failure as a broken promise and breach of trust and felt "ashamed" to approach the bird again. His defeat conforms with his overall impression of Chichester, a place where all free spirits are desecrated, where calves are led to slaughter, where everything has been reduced to soot and decay, and permeated by an acrid stench.

Hudson also railed against the collectors who took lives in order to put dead forms on display. In *Hampshire Days* Hudson tells of his meeting with the vicar of a small parish who calls himself a "lepidopterist." Hudson tells this man of his own admiration for the humming-bird hawk-moth he once saw "suspended on his misty wings among the tall flowers in the brilliant August sunshine," and tries in vain to convey the beauty and thrill the sight inspired in him.[42] The lepidopterist dryly remarks that "the season had not proved a very good one for the *Macroglossa Stellatarum*" and describes his own adventure securing such a specimen without a net.[43] Hudson closes with a final sketch of this religionist blind to the magic of living things: "I cannot imagine him in that beautiful country of the Future . . . in white raiment, with a golden harp in his hand; for if here, in *this* country, he could see nothing in a humming-bird hawk-moth among the flowers in the sunshine but an object to be collected, what in the name of wonder will he have to harp about!"[44]

Not just in these travel books, but in his reading of newspapers and periodicals Hudson was on the look out for opportunities to strike out against the mistreatment of animals. The most notable of these occurred in 1900 when Hudson jumped to the defense of the albatross after twin articles appeared in *Nature* which describe the then popular custom on ships of putting the bird through a series of tortures in order to find out how much agony it could endure. The first article tells of "an albatross supposed to have been choked dead, kept in an ice box at a temperature which was always much below freezing point" that "was found to be alive at the end of fourteen days."[45] When the article caught Hudson's eye, he composed a letter published in *The Saturday Review* on November 24, 1900 which begins with a picture of the bird alive in its natural habitat:

> The mere sight of this noble pelagic fowl, the great wandering albatross is a moving event in the life of any person, even as is that of the soaring condor among his native mountains;

31

and, in a less degree, that of the golden eagle, the one great bird which happily still survives in the northernmost parts of our country.

From there Hudson reverts to his method of contrast by denouncing the Philistine who could take any such lord from its proper kingdom and sentence it to an inquisition and untimely death. In his battle Hudson was joined by his compatriot, Cunninghame Graham, who sent in his own letter which was published in the same paper on December 1, 1900.

Hudson also employed newspapers and magazines as outlets for his anger against the feathered women, the English socialites parading about with corpses pinned to their frocks. In "The Feather Fashion: A Last Word" printed in *The Humane Review* in January 1901, Hudson claims to be plagued by "the daily sight of innumerable carcasses and wings and feathers of birds that were once beautiful—most beautiful of all earth's inhabitants—now hideous to see, dead and discoloured and crushed out of shape, their brilliant living wild eyes replaced by glass and crockery beads."[46] In the essay, "Feathered Women," addressed to the editor of *The Times* on October 17, 1893, in a "Letter to Clergymen, Ministers and Others," sent out in November 1895, and in "The Trade in Bird's Feathers," also to the editor of *The Times* printed on December 25, 1897, Hudson graphically presents the finery itself and connects the trend with savage practices, with the ornaments on "the naked female savage of Venezuela" or the "necklace of human ears (captured from the enemy) which a Mexican lady is said to have exhibited in a ballroom."[47] The English practices engendered by this fashion are just as barbaric because "the fowlers in their haste do not stop to kill the wounded birds, but merely wrench the wings off, and cast the birds back to die in slow agony on the water."[48] In these tracts Hudson links the "murderous millinery" to cannibal headdresses, emphasizes the heathenism of

Christians, and laments the results, the extinction of many divine species in England.

Hudson, the preservationist, did not limit himself to the protection of animals. As is evident in his plea to save Land's End, he extended his reverence to the land and vegetation. In "An Old Thorn" Hudson gives us an example of tree worship and tells the story of Johnnie Budd who in an attempt to rescue his dependents from starvation, steals sheep, undergoes a severe trial and receives the death sentence. On the surface the story seems to be a critique of the old rural judicial system, a theme which also surfaces in *A Shepherd's Life*. But beneath this is the real message—don't hurt trees. Hudson begins the tale with a portrait of the deity, "a small solitary tree standing near the summit—an old thorn with ivy growing on it."[49] The narrator, who feels himself mysteriously drawn to the thorn and senses within its branches a conscious life, a history, inquires amongst the villagers of the South Wiltshire Downs in hopes of obtaining some information. After several thwarted attempts to learn about the venerable tree, he discovers that it played a key part in the tragic execution of Johnnie Budd. As a child Budd and a playmate, his future wife, climbed the old thorn and injured its branches. A stranger instantly appeared on the scene to deliver the ominous warning, "something will come out of it and follow you wherever you go and hurt and break you at last."[50] Directly before his execution Johnnie is haunted by the vision of the tree and the words of its guardian. Although Hudson leads us to sympathize with the young offender and feel his sentence is much too harsh for the actual crime, the theft of sheep, he also convinces us that Budd's fate is retribution for his real crime against Nature.

Because Hudson's activities as preservationist dominated such a major portion of his life, it is nearly impossible to put these works in a class all their own. Even if it meant disrupting the flow of his narrative, Hudson could not resist inserting into his novels statements against the abuse of wildlife. For example, in *A Crystal Age*, Smith, the Englishman who awakens to find himself in utopia, wonders at the flock of birds and suddenly delivers the author's diatribe: "yet it was not strange that birds were so abundant, considering that there were no longer any savages on the earth, with nothing to amuse their vacant minds except killing the feathered creatures with their bows and arrows, and no innumerable company of squaws clamourous for trophies—unchristian women of the woods with painted faces, insolence in their eyes, and for ornaments the feathered skins torn from slain birds on their heads."[51] Likewise, the heroes and heroines in Hudson's books are either humanitarians or new converts to the worship of Nature and the defense of her creatures. After all, Rima divested of her unearthliness looks a lot like a fanatical member of the Humanitarian League, a vegetarian martyred by a band of blood-thristy carnivores. The pastoral Caleb Bawcombe wins Hudson's heart because he studies birds as an aside and rescues a lark from imprisonment; Yoletta, Smith's beloved, attaches herself spiritually to the entire feathered world. Even Fan, the city girl, when granted leisure time, observes wild life in the country and opts for outdoor study over and above her tutorials in the house.

It is surprising that this ardent protector of wild life began his career in South America as a hunter and collector of birds. While Hudson was growing up on the pampas he prepared and sent bird skins to Dr. Spencer Fullerton Baird, assistant secretary of the Smithsonian Institution, and even made his mark by discovering a new species, named *cnipolegus hudsoni*, the tyrant-bird, described fully in *Birds of La Plata*.[52] Once Hudson arrived in England his collecting days were done and he seldom mentioned his early transgressions, his own search for specimens. It is likely that this change in attitude began in Patagonia in 1871 when a wound in the knee from an accidental shot from a friend's gun confined him to inactivity for several months. Being immobilized in that "solitary wilderness" pulled Hudson away from his purely scientific orientation and nurtured his spiritual and aesthetic sense of Nature.[53] In England Hudson's change was finalized when he found comrades and whole organizations to support him in his efforts to express his profound reverence for life.

There was nothing Hudson wouldn't sacrifice for his cause: he was willing to retract the veil of anonymity around *Fan*, a novel for which he felt little regard, just to raise money for the Bird Society. In later life, he expressed regret to Morley Roberts that he never employed an agent who might have obtained higher prices for his books and earned more money for his cause.[54] At the end of his life, when Emily's death preceded his, Hudson left his entire estate to the Bird Society, an intention explained to Roberts in a letter of 1918.[55]

Even though Hudson did adjust to life in London, he undeniably felt a degree of homesickness and frequently drifted off into the past. As late as 1900 Hudson confessed to temporary displacements in time: "By the bye, when I am going a distance on the wheel I sometimes drop into the idea that I am on horseback, and only recover consciousness of the different sort of wild beast I am astride of when it begins to fly down a long slope."[56] As a writer Hudson learned to make use of these moments where past and present converge. He believed that a naturalist fixes upon the subject, describes it, and then gives the imagination free reign. The mind can transform the present into a vision of the future or wind back to a scene from childhood. This way time becomes an open plain which can be crossed or retraced at will, where a writer can hike from the English downs to the South American pampas in one sentence. A clear example of this journey through time occurs in the opening of *Nature in Downland*.

It was not only that the sight was beautiful, but the scene was vividly reminiscent of long-gone summer days associated in

35

memory with the silvery thistle-down. The wide extent of unenclosed and untilled earth, its sunburnt colour and its solitariness, when no person was in sight; the vast void blue sky, with no mist nor cloud on it; the burning sun and wind and the sight of thousands upon thousands of balls or stars of down reminded me of old days on horseback on the open pampa—an illimitable waste of rust-red thistles, and the sky above covered with its million floating flecks of white.[57]

Hudson's descriptions of Argentina are not always these nostalgic glimpses at beauty and freedom. In *Hampshire Days* the spectacle before him evokes a recollection of violence. The naturalist watches two flies in combat: "they locked together, and I saw the attacking insect raise his head and fore part of his body so as to strike, then plunge his rostrum like a dagger in the soft part of his victim's body. Again and again he raised and buried his weapon on the other, and the other still refusing to die or to cease struggling."[58] After beholding this dipteran battle, Hudson becomes aware of a "feeling of intense repugnance" which was "wholly due to association." He searches his memory and unearths a scene of human combat witnessed in youth: "the dagger-like weapon and the action of the insect were curiously human-like, and I had seen just such a combat between two men, one fallen and the other on him, raising and striking down with his knife." Hudson does not just describe the scene, but makes the entire experience into an example of the mnemonic creative process: " had I never witnessed such an incident, the two flies struggling, one killing the other would have produced no such feeling, and would not have been remembered." He explained that time does not rule the mind, but that "we live in thoughts and feelings, not in days and years." He again demonstrates the workings of the associational process when the mere sight of a hornet causes him to relive the pain experienced as a child when he tried to capture an intruder. First he announces his respect for the European wasp before him, then connects this with the recent past, the gesture of the parson-lepidopterist sweeping to grab a creature in flight, and finally revives the most receded memory of the boyhood trauma when the wasp "succeeded in curling his abdomen" around, and planted his long sting in the sensitive tip of [his] forefinger."[59]

Hudson often used these equations between his present life in England and a past image of South America to enrich the scene before him. In *The Land's End* Hudson visits St. Ives in Cornwall and shares the ritual with his readers, the fishermen uniting with their boats in the harbor for their evening's work.

> The best spectacle is when they are taken out at or near sunset in fair weather, when the subdued light gives a touch of tenderness and mystery to sea and sky, and the boats singly, in twos and threes, and in groups of half a dozen, drift out from the harbour and go away in a kind of procession over the sea.[60]

Hudson watching this night after night, senses that there is something most familiar about these shapes and tones, and attributes this "to association—to vague suggestions of a resemblance in this to other scenes." He searches his memory for the original image which has infused the scene with grace and splendor, and arrives at a past event, the movement of a community of birds at rest in shallow waters:

> By-and-by one of the birds steps out of a crowd and moves leisurely away, then slowing and unfolding his broad wings, launches himself on the air and goes off, flying very low over the water. Another follows, then, after an interval, another, then still others, in twos and threes and half-dozens, until the last bird has opened his wings and the entire flock is seen moving away in a loose procession over the lake.

This boyhood memory leads to the interlacement of a metaphor: "just in that way did the crowd of boats move by degrees from their resting-place, shake out their wing-like sails, and stream away over the sea." These temporary retrospections enrich the scenes before him.

Hudson's most prolonged journey back in time is his own autobiography. The rough draft of *Far Away and Long Ago* came to life in Cornwall in 1916 when Hudson was convalescing in a convent hospital and claimed to have seen his entire past unravel before him like a film on the screen of his mind.

> It was not like that mental condition, known to some persons when some sight or sound or, more frequently, the perfume of some flower, associated with our early life, restores the past suddenly and so vividly that it is almost an illusion. That is an intensely emotional condition and vanishes as quickly as it comes. This was different. To return to the simile and metaphor used at the beginning, it was as if the cloud shadows and haze had passed away and the entire prospect beneath me made clearly visible.[61]

Hudson, wishing to immortalize this epiphany, propped up with pillows, put his confinement to work by writing an account of his early years. As a whole, *Far Away and Long Ago* best demonstrates Hudson's skill at wedding past with present and reveals his refusal to be artistically controlled by sequential time.

Becoming a British subject in 1900 was a decision Hudson never regretted. Even when finances improved, he rarely extended his travels outside the country, except for a short visit to Ireland. He made no attempt to return to Argentina or visit his younger sister who stayed there until her death in 1919. England provided Hudson with everything he needed for his work: he continued his war against urbanization, explored new countryside, and protested against the abuse of wildlife. But beyond this, England gave Hudson the necessary distance from South America which enabled him to interweave past and present most effectively. When Sydney Smith of *A Crystal Age* meets with the utopian hive, he announces chauvinistically "My country is England, and my name is Smith."[62] There is no doubt that Hudson is speaking, at least momentarily, from behind the mask of this proud patriot.

CHAPTER III

Hudson's People
—Real and Imaginary

ON JULY 31, 1913, William Henry Hudson explained to Morley Roberts that he is not the first to accuse him of being an impenetrable mystery: "What you say about not knowing me reminds me of the very last words my favourite brother (now dead) said to me when we parted on the boat: 'Of all the people I know you are the only one I have never known.'"[1] The Hudson of Roberts's *Portrait* and in the sketches by various acquaintances is an enigma, a man who kept himself apart from the human race, a man who communed more easily with animals than with people, a man who frequently burned letters and documents to insure his secrecy and to avoid post-mortem publicity.

Hudson's contemporaries found Hudson's marriage as puzzling as the man himself. It was difficult, if not impossible, for those who knew him to believe that such a detached character could have a stable marriage. Sir William Rothenstein, who in 1916 painted Hudson's portrait which is displayed in the National Portrait Gallery, recounts a conversation with Hudson and summarizes what he believed to be a waning relationship.

It was some time before we discovered that he was married. One day he spoke of his wife, 'Married!' said my wife, 'And you never told us! How long have you been married?' 'As long as I can remember,' was Hudson's answer, the gloomiest verdict on married life I have ever heard. He had met, early in life, a singer, a friend of Adelina Patti, with a great career before her; in love with her and her voice, he induced her to marry him. Then something happened; she lost her voice and was never to sing again, the tragedy for both of them.[2]

Similarly, Ford Madox Ford recalls a conversation between himself, Joseph Conrad and Edward Garnett which sums up some of the legends and rumors circulating about Hudson and his minute consort.

Conrad would dilate with enthusiasm about this *capataz* of the Revolution who had a wife as tiny as he was romantic. 'You know,' he would say, 'she's so tiny that when she stands on the floor she cannot look over the edge of the dinner table. Extraordinary!' And Mr. Garnett would add information about Mrs. Hudson's exquisite voice; about her having been the rival of Jenny Lind and of Malibran of Her Majesty's opera, and of her having wilfully refused to sing a note after he married her . . . so that there was the tragedy of Rima of *Green Mansions* all over again.[3]

Violet Hunt also failed to see much joy in this marriage and in her accounts she lashes out at a woman she never had the opportunity to meet—"a witch of German legend, this Rapunzel, sitting there in her tower, her short legs propped up on a huge footstool, claiming the constant society of her distinguished husband who, then, was not making money."[4] From hearsay alone Hunt knows all about this "tiny being possessed of a mighty voice, who long before she went had grown sulky and cantankerous; made pettish demands on his time and his patience, and kept his friends away from the house."[5] She is certain that Hudson did not love Emily, but stood by her out of a sense of duty and honor.

Emily Wingrave was more than a shadow or nagging obligation in Hudson's life. This woman had a strength and life all her own. In her heyday she had become a fairly successful soprano and appeared on stage several times with other stars. When her voice began to fail, she supported herself by teaching music and operating the boarding-house. When she married Hudson she not only provided him with food and shelter during his dark years, but also gave him unfailing companionship. The Hudsons had many interests in common: they enjoyed the same books, they both loved birds and the outdoors, and they valued their walks through the countryside. Before Emily's health began to deteriorate, this woman who was fifteen to twenty years older than her husband, accompanied him on his rustic excursions. In *Afoot in England* Hudson explains with warmth and humor how the two of them coexisted on their journeys.

> I would leave her half a mile or so behind to force my way through unkept hedges, climb hills, and explore woods and thickets to converse with every bird and shy little beast and scaly creature I could discover. But mark what follows. In the late afternoon I would be back in the road or footpath, satisfied to go slow, then slower still, until the snail in woman shape would be obliged to slacken her pace to keep me company, and even to stand still at intervals to give me needful rest.[6]

Apparently the Hudsons evolved their own symbiosis for these journeys that supplied him with raw material for his books. Ford Madox Ford confirms the fact that the two were often seen together, "going away toward English greennesses, through the most lugubrious streets the world could imagine, let alone know; and Huddie would be expressing theories as to the English rain and far below him his tiny wife would be in-

cessantly telling him that he was going the wrong way."[7]
Hudson willingly sacrificed the liberty and solitude he enjoyed
so he could include Emily on these outings, and she, in turn,
gave up the comforts of home. Hudson frequently declared his
love for Emily in his books. In "The Return of the Chiff-Chaff"
he remembers her guiding him "waist-deep in the flowering
meadow grasses," and then says, "that bond uniting us, unlike
all other bonds, was unbreakable and everlasting."[8]

When Emily became so ill she could no longer accompany
him, Hudson stayed home a great deal and attended her with
patience. Violet Hunt describes how "at the stroke of six,
Huddie would put down his cup, or whatever he was holding,
and bolt back to her."[9] In the years before Emily's death when
she lived with a nurse at West Taring, he wrote to her every day
and visited her as often as possible. His concern comes across
clearly in a letter to Roberts from Penzance dated March 1921:
"I am too unwell and in a most anxious state about my wife,
who is unconscious and sinking, but Dr. Miller tells me I am
not fit to travel, so must wait here."[10] It is clear from letters and
passages in his books that Hudson's marriage was important to
him. There is also no doubt that in Emily were combined the
elements that most appealed to Hudson—a child-like appearance, a bird-like voice, and an adult capacity to share his life
and work.

Although Hudson was socially selective, he did, partially
through the efforts of Edward Garnett, build up a literary following and cultivate numerous friendships in London. Edward
Garnett who knew Hudson for approximately twenty-one years
recalls his first encounter with an exceptionally tall man who
walked into his office on his last day as Heinemann's reader, a
writer who was most eager to establish a tie with one of the first
to express admiration for his work.

Some weeks before I had impressed on Mr. William Heinemann that *El Ombú* was a work of genius and that he must

43

publish it. 'But we shan't sell it!' objected Mr. William Heinemann in his nervous, excitable fashion. He had temporized, afraid either to return the MS or to accept it, and now Hudson had come to learn his decision. I went up to Hudson and told him that he had written a masterpiece. Its grave beauty, its tragic sweetness, indeed, had swept me off my feet, as it does now when I read it. Hudson glared at me astonished, as though he wished to annihilate me and asked my name. I told him, adding, 'It's my last day here. Where can I meet you?' Suddenly his face changed and he said, 'Let's go and find a place to lunch.'[11]

Hudson proceeded to the Mont Blanc Restaurant on Gerrard Street with Edward Garnett, who later when he became the reader for Duckworth arranged for the publication of *El Ombú* in the Greenback Library. Hudson continued lunching at the Mont Blanc with Garnett every Tuesday, and this ritual brought him in contact with other writers—Thomas Seccombe, R.A. Scott James, Stephen Reynolds, W.H. Davies, Hilaire Belloc, Muirhead Bone, Ford Madox Ford, Perceval Gibbon, John Galsworthy, Joseph Conrad, and Edward Thomas.

Hudson enjoyed being in communication with the younger set of writers, especially Edward Thomas, who shared his appreciation for Richard Jefferies and Burton's *Anatomy of Melancholy*.[12] Apparently Edward Thomas came to idolize Hudson and view his writings as models. Hudson's reciprocated affection comes across in his expressed remorse over his sudden and premature death. In April 1917 Hudson explains the tragedy to Morley Roberts:

Alas! My poor young friend, Edward Thomas—writer of many books and reviews of poetry in *The Nation* and some newspapers, has just been killed . . . Poor Thomas hated war and when he found they would not send him out because he was too useful in teaching map-reading to young officers (when he was in the infantry) he petitioned to be allowed to go with the artillery, and after six months training on Salisbury Plain went out about five months ago and met his end in the great Arias battle. He leaves a young wife and two children and they were wholly dependent on his literary earnings for a livelihood.[13]

Throughout his life Hudson never forgot this friendship, and in 1922 he began the introduction to a collection of Thomas's essays, *Cloud Castle and Other Papers*, which was his last project. In the unfinished foreword he calls Thomas "one of the most lovable beings."[14]

In addition to friendships with other writers, Hudson made a point of forming friendships with others who had ties with South America or with other distant lands. Hudson relished his luncheons with Wilfrid Scawen Blunt, the poet and travel writer, who published pamphlets supporting the nationalist cause in India, Arabia, Egypt, and Ireland, a man "who had the most amusing adventures to relate of his time in the Banda Orientál when he was a young attaché of the legation in Buenos Aires 35 or 40 years ago."[15] Hudson also maintained a close relationship with R.B. Cunninghame Graham, who sometimes seemed to be a misplaced gaucho as he rode his horse in the Row in London. In addition to Don Roberto who also knew the pampas, Hudson communicated with Rabindranath Tagore, the Indian playwright, novelist, painter, educator and musician, with T.E. Lawrence, almost a myth himself, "Lawrence of Arabia," whom Hudson described to Roberts on June 16, 1919:

I found him arrayed in the most beautiful male dress of the East I have ever seen—a reddish camel-hair mantle or cloak with gold collar over a white gown reaching to the ground, and a white headpiece with 3 silver cords or ropes round it. . . . He is a worshipper of Doughty and also told me he had read *The Purple Land* 12 times. . . . It struck me that *The Purple Land* was just the sort of book that would appeal to a young adventurer like Lawrence—a sort of Richard Lamb himself.[16]

Hudson valued his relationship with other nature-lovers and members of the Bird Society. When he wasn't meeting with Linda Gardiner, Wynnard Hooper, Ernest Bell, Mrs. Frank E. Lemon, Lord Grey and his wife, Dorothy, Hudson was paying visits to people on bird protection errands. Ford Madox Ford who attempted to soothe his nerves after a mental breakdown filled his room with African wax-billed finches and parakeets. He describes Hudson's inspection of the conditions:

> At that he came to see me and stumped up the stairs to inspect my bedroom. He looked for a long time at the birds which were perfectly lively. Then he recommended me to have some large mirrors set into the walls with perches in front of them. And to hang about bright silvered balls from Christmas trees, and scarlet ribbons. Birds, he said, loved all bright objects, and the mirrors gave them the illusion, with their reflected images, that they were in great crowds of birds. Then he said, 'Humph,' and stumped down the stairs and never to me mentioned the subject of birds in captivity again.[17]

In his own letters when Hudson is not describing these bird-missions which he took quite seriously, or giving his correspondent a careful count of each and every heart beat during one of his many illnesses, he is waiting for the Ranee of Sarawak to arrive in her car or dashing off to make an appointment. On June 25 Hudson gives Roberts a glimpse at a rather typical schedule:

> I fear I can't make any lunching engagement as I have accepted several invitations for the week. Monday I have to meet Garnett and perhaps someone else in the evening. I have also to go to the Strand that day. Next day either Massingham or

Dr. Parson, the director of the Audubon Societies, and the other on Wednesday.[18]

On top of these many meetings, Hudson carried on an immense correspondence right up until his death and periodically burned stacks of letters. In April 1906 Hudson tells Garnett that "if [he] had preserved all the letters worth keeping since [he] came to England they would now number not less than twenty thousand."[19]

In addition to his involvement with people in his day to day life, Hudson included a most interesting assortment of characters in his books. Most frequently Hudson's people live in close contact with the outdoors or engage in some form of spiritual communion with the wilds: these are the wandering vagabonds, shepherds, farmers, peasants and gauchos all sketched against their larger environments.

In *Far Away and Long Ago* Hudson brings to life the unconventional men and women living on the outskirts of civilization. These are individuals who lend themselves to natural imagery, characters whose distinguishing features seem analogous to elements in their environments. In the first chapter, "Earliest Memories," we meet Captain Scott, a visiting Englishman, "an immense man, with a great round face of a purplish-red colour, like the sun setting in glory, and surrounded with a fringe of silvery-white hair and whiskers, standing out like the petals round the disc of a sunflower."[20] Another character, the hermit, a kind of Ahasuerus, roams about the countryside and lives apart from any community.

> Money he always refused with gestures of intense disgust, and he would also decline cooked meat and broken bread. When hard biscuits were given him, he would carefully examine them, and if one was found chipped or cracked he would return it, pointing out the defect, and ask for a sound one in return. He had a small, sun-parched face, and silvery long hair; but his features were fine, his teeth white and even,

his eyes clear grey and keen as a falcon's.[21]

Although in retrospect Hudson perceives a "touch of insanity," he regards this vagabond as a symbol of rebellion against regimentation and the norms of civilization.

The autobiography is filled with the unusual and grotesque: the blind beggar on horseback "who galloped about the land collecting tribute from the people and talking loftily about the powers above;"[22] the mystery of the "huge, ox-like man" who fell into the moat and was brought back from the dead by a rescue party;[23] Dona Pascuala who smoked cigars and punished St. Anthony for the oppressive rainstorms by submerging his image in a well;[24] the Patriarch Barboza "with fierce eagle-like eyes under bushy black eyebrows that looked like tufts of feather" whose "chief glory was an immense crow-black beard"; Mr. Royd who insisted on making cheese from sheep's milk, and who suddenly passed into the clouds of depression and "committed suicide by cutting his throat with a razor";[25] Don Gregorio with "a round or barrel-shaped body, short bow legs, and a big round head" who owned a pet ostrich and bred only piebald horses";[26] Don Anastacio, "an ineffectual, colourless, effeminate person" who "cherished an affection" for wild pigs;[27] Jack the Killer, "one of those strange Englishmen . . . who had taken to the gaucho manner of life" and fought off seven armed men with only a small knife.[28]

Out of the complete catalogue of extraordinary people, Don Evaristo Peñalva, a "patriarch of the pampas" and major landowner, stands out as Hudson's best example of a man who lives entirely by his own laws. Hudson describes the six wives all living under one roof:

> The first, the only one he had been permitted to marry in a church, was old as or rather older than himself; she was very dark and was getting wrinkles, and was the mother of several grown-up sons and daughters, some married. The others were of various ages, the youngest two about thirty; and these

were twin sisters both named Ascension, for they were born on Ascension Day.[29]

Don Evaristo, a master of many arts, a sage, a medicine man with the only sure cure for the shingles, is not condemned or even judged by his neighbors for his polygamy.

> If it pleased such a man as that to have six wives instead of one, it was right and proper for him to have them; no person would presume to say that he was not a good and wise and religious man on that account. It may be added that Don Evaristo, like Henry VIII, who also had six wives, was a strictly virtuous man. The only difference was that when he desired a fresh wife he did not barbarously execute or put away the one, or the others, he already possessed.[30]

In *Far Away and Long Ago* Hudson writes entirely within the unique perspective of the pampas' laws. He refuses to impose on his characters any rules or morals outside this world. The inhabitants live in harmony with the wilds and refuse to conform to any modern standards of morality.

In books on English countryside Hudson also seeks to protray anachronistic individuals. The old woman of *Hampshire Days* who lives by selling the produce of her garden resists progress by faithfully clinging to her elderberry wine rituals.

> I've made elderberry wine years and years and years. So did my mother; so did my grandmother; so did everybody in *my* time. And very good it were, too, I tell'ee, in cold weather in winter, made hot. It warmed your inside. But nobody wants it now, and nobody'll help me with it. . . . Nothing's good enough now unless you buys it in a public house or a shop. It wasn't so when I were a girl.[31]

At the close of her speech in which she contrasts a more natural past with the artificiality of the present, she turns to a new subject, the song of birds which to her suggests a consoling constancy amidst the turmoil of change.

> And my mother she used to say, 'Lord how she do love to hear a blackbird!' It's always the same. I's always up at four, and in the summer I goes out to hear the blackbird when it do sing so beautifully. . . . But things is very different now; and what I say is, I wish they wasn't—I wish they was the same as when I were a girl. And I wish I was a girl again.[32]

To Hudson this woman with her "tirade on the degeneracy of modern times" is "one of the best examples of the hard-headed indomitable peasants," a being close to Nature and the ways of a glorious past.

Hudson's portrait of the vicar in *Afoot in England* is one of the finest examples of how he transferred his flair for the strange and singular from South America to the characters living in rural England. The clergyman who "kept his gravity even when he said things which would have gone very well with a smile" has an almost indefinable eccentricity as he relates the story of his first church and its resident Batrachians.[33]

> You smile, sir, but it was no smiling matter for me during my first year as vicar, when I discovered that it was the custom here to keep pet toads in the church. It sounds strange and funny, no doubt, but it is a fact that all the best people in the parish had one of these creatures, and it was customary for the ladies to bring it a weekly supply of provisions—bits of meat, hard boiled eggs chopped up, and earth-worms, and whatever else they fancied it would like—in their reticules. The toads, I suppose, knew when it was Sunday—their feeding day; at all events they would crawl out of their holes in the floor under the pews to receive their rations and caresses.[34]

Later when Hudson steps aside from this story and removes himself from the spell of this peculiar man, he decides it was "one of the oddest incidents" of his life, and this he attributes to a "sense of something strange in the mind."[35] In the close of the incident Hudson walks away with a vision of "an effigy of a semi-human toad-like creature smiling down mockingly at the worshippers as they came and went," which for him becomes an emblem of the oddness of everyday life.[36]

Also in *Afoot in England* Hudson exposes a way of life antithetical to urban existence. Mrs. Flowerdew, a landlady, agrees to let the Hudsons a room for the night even though she had been forced to sell her furniture to pay for her husband's debts. The whole community joins together in a common goal—to supply the necessary provisions.

> We formed the idea that her neighbours must have been her debtors for unnumbered little kindnesses, so eager did they now appear to do her a good turn. Out of one cottage a woman was seen coming burdened with a big roll of bedding; from others children issued bearing cane chairs, basin and ewer, and so on, and when we next looked into our room we found it swept and scrubbed, mats on the floor and quite comfortably furnished.[37]

Not only does this community represent the rustic ideal, humanity at peace with nature, at peace with each other, but Mr. Flowerdew who returns in the evening embodies all the qualities that Hudson held sacred. His description of this man is an indirect commentary on the dying art of seeing clearly and of living completely.

> Certainly this white-haired man had not grown old in mind; he was keenly interested in all he saw and heard, and he had seen and heard much in the little market town that day. Cattle and pigs and sheep and shepherds and sheepdogs; farmers, shopkeepers, dealers, publicans, tramps and gentlefolks in carriages and on horseback; shops, too, with beautiful new things in the windows; millinery, agricultural implements, flowers and fruit and vegetables; toys and books and sweeties of all colours. And the people he had met on the road and at market, and what they said to him about the weather and their business and the prospects of the year, how

their wives and children were, and the clever jokes they had made, and his own jokes, which were cleverest of all.[38]

Mr. Flowerdew does not require the obvious or exotic to excite his imagination—"if he had just returned from Central Africa or from Thibet, he could not have had more to tell them nor told it with greater zest."[39] This man and his communal world represent humanity at its best.

The individual who stands out because of his sense of freedom appears for a moment in *A Shepherd's Life*. Although he bolts through the marketplace at Salisbury and comes to life for a mere two pages, he becomes more fascinating than Caleb Bawcomb, the real hero and focal point of the book. This character who catches the narrator's eye is "a young man of about twenty-two or twenty-three, a shepherd in a grey suit and thick, iron shod, old boots and brown leggings, with a soft, felt hat thrust jauntily on the back of his head, coming along . . . with that half slouching, half-swinging gait peculiar to the men of the downs especially when they are in town on pleasure bent."[40] Hudson describes this man in depth and his impact on the crowd which also senses his singularity and stares after him. As Hudson narrows in on this individual he comes to resemble a wild creature, a reflection of the soul within Nature itself.

> As he came on I placed myself directly in his path and stared straight into his eyes—grey eyes and very beautiful; but he refused to see me; he stared through me like an animal when you try to catch its eyes, and went by still trolling out his song, with all the others streaming after him.[41]

This charismatic shepherd of the downs represents the ideal: he projects an independence and detachment similar to the elusive qualities Abel perceives in Rima when she is darting through the woods.

Her eyes were wide open, gazing fixedly before her; and

when I looked into them they seemed to see and yet not to see me. They were like the clear, brilliant eyes of a bird, which reflect as in a miraculous mirror all the visible world but do not return our look and seem to see us merely as one of the thousand small details that make up the whole picture.[42]

The shepherd, like Rima, lives in perfect accord with nature and has come to radiate an untamed beauty.

Although Hudson does not ennoble the savage, who as Abel discovers, lives by the lower, carnivorous laws of nature, he is intrigued with the individual who leaves civilization to become part of a more primitive culture. In *Idle Days in Patagonia* he relates the history of Damian, who when only a boy saves himself by pretending to detest his own white race and joining the enemy, the Indians. They teach him to "share in the simple delights of the aborigines," and force him to endure those "long hunting expeditions in the depth of winter, exposed all day to bitter cold and furious storms of wind and sleet, cursed and beaten for his awkwardness by his fellow-huntsmen";[43] he learns to drink blood "hot from the heart of the still living brute" and partake of the "grand annual drinking bouts."[44] After Damian becomes "fluent in their language, and outwardly in all things like a savage," and marries an Indian who bears him children, he begins to long for contact with his own lost race. When he does return to the white settlement thirty years later he is not welcomed since "exposure to the sun and wind of the desert had made him so brown, while in manner and speech he had grown like an Indian."[45] Hudson reflects upon this total solitude and sympathizes with the grief of the abandoned Indian woman.

There was something pathetic in the life of that poor returned wanderer, an alien now to his own fellow-townsmen, homeless amidst the pleasant vineyards, poplar groves, and old stone houses where he had first seen the light. . . . Possibly also, the memory of his savage spouse who had loved him many years would add some bitterness to his strange isolated life. For far away from their old home, she would still wait for him, vainly hoping, fearing much, dim eyed with sorrow and long watching, yet never seeing his form returning to her out of the mysterious haze of the desert.[46]

Although nonconformism fascinated Hudson, he was careful never to romanticize total isolation or exile. The ideal individual is moderate: he can integrate a life in nature with participation in the finer things of civilization. He is not estranged like the semi-savage Damian who must live like a leper apart from the community, but instead liberated like the shepherd of the downs who although detached and somewhat wild, still retains ties with town and family.

In his fantasy writing Hudson often created characters who were fusions of animal life and humanity. In *A Little Boy Lost*, a children's book which appeared in 1905, Hudson strives to obliterate the distinction between man and beast in order to communicate a vision of an intelligence in Nature. Martin, a unique and restless child, wanders away from his parents and meets with a series of supernatural adventures: vultures descend as little men in dark suits; the hills become a lady in a green dress; and the sea is portrayed as an illusive old man "with a vast, snow-white beard, and a world of disordered white hair floating over and round its head."[47] The most perfect hybrid of man-brute appears in the chapter, "A Troop of Wild Horses," where Martin meets the tribe leader.

> As they galloped by, he caught sight of the strangest looking being he had ever seen, a man on the back of one of the horses; naked and hairy, he looked like a baboon as he crouched, doubled up, gripping the shoulders and neck of the horse with his knees, clinging with his hands to the mane, and craning his neck like a flying bird. It was this strange rider who had uttered the long piercing man-and-bird like

cries; and now changing his voice to a whinnying sound the horses came to a stop.[48]

This human stallion appears as various and ever-changing as Nature itself: he becomes man, baboon, bird and horse as he guides the boy into a wild life of unceasing movement and speed.

Aside from Martin, Hudson included a vast assortment of little girls in his works: these young characters often symbolize the purity, the magic and delight of a natural life removed from the drawing room of the adult. The Hudson of the essays frequently courts or vows love to some little temptress.[49] In "Millicent and Another," a chapter from *A Traveller in Little Things*, Hudson finds himself caught in a love triangle where he chooses the younger lover, the four-year old Mab, over the six-year old Millicent. Hudson begins his romantic adventure with a sketch of Millicent and a synopsis of their interactions which are always tight and restrained: she was "tall for her years, straight and slim, with no red colour on her cheeks; she had brown hair and large serious grey eyes; those eyes and her general air of gravity, and her forehead, which was too broad for perfect beauty made me a little shy of her and we were not too intimate."[50] One evening he and Millicent are walking hand-in-hand when she breaks through the silence with a sudden declaration of love:

> I shall never forget that morning when you went away last time. . . . It was early in the morning and I was in bed. You know how late I always am. I heard you calling to me to come down and say goodbye; so I jumped up and came down in my night dress and saw you standing waiting for me at the foot of the stairs. Then, when I got down, you took me up in your arms and kissed me. I shall never forget it.[51]

When Hudson fails to respond, Millicent, who is clever and prematurely skilled in manipulative tactics, introduces the jeal-

55

ous competitor: "that day after school I saw Uncle Charlie and told him, and he said: 'What! You allowed that tramp to kiss you! Then I don't want to take you on my knee any more—you've lowered yourself too much.' " This does not excite a reply from the narrator who is then thinking of his preferred sweetheart, "one who was also a person of importance in her own home and village over a dozen miles away," the more spontaneous Mab, "a child of earth and sun, exquisite, with her flossy hair a shining chestnut gold, eyes like the bugloss, her whole face like a flower or rather like a ripe peach in bloom and colour."[52] After a breathless description of this child's inexhaustible energy and curiosity, he explains why he and Mab were the only wise spectators that didn't cry at a village funeral:

> Our tearless condition—our ability to keep dry when it was raining, so to say—resulted from quite different causes. Mine just then were the eyes of a naturalist curiously observing the demeanor of the beings around me. To Mab the whole spectacle was an act, an interlude, or scene in that wonderful endless play which was a perpetual delight to witness and in which she too was taking a part.[53]

Hudson then leaves behind their funeral date to comment on the ephemerality of this kind of loveliness and innocence:

> I would not spoil that lovely image by going back to look at her again. Three years! It was said of Lewis Carroll that he ceased to care anything about his little Alices when they had come to the age of ten. Seven is my limit: they are perfect then: but in Mab's case the peculiar exquisite charm could hardly have lasted beyond the age of six.

Hudson's attraction for little girls, his stated preference for Mab's candor over Millicent's cunning, serve to point out the beauty of human nature that has not yet acquired the disguises of experience.

In *A Traveller in Little Things* Hudson sketches one miniature portrait after another: the "sturdy little thing of about five years old, in heavy clothes and cloth cap, and long knitted muffler wrapped around her neck" who "drew away to the opposite side of the road, thinking that so big a man would require the whole of its twenty-five yards' width for himself";[54] the spinning top who "came dancing out from among the tea-drinkers" and "whirled, heedless of the presence of all those people, happy and free and wild as a lamb running a race with itself on some green flowery down under the wide sky."[55] Later he devotes most of a chapter to a little girl, Freckles, whom he met in a country town in the West of England, a child he loves for her mind, not her beauty. He begins with a description of her peculiar appearance:

> Her head, big for her size and years, was as perfectly round as a Dutch cheese, and her face so thickly freckled that it was all freckles; she had confluent freckles, and as the spots and blotches were of different shades, one could see that they overlapped like the scales of a fish. Her head was bound tightly round with a piece of white calico, and no hair appeared under it.[56]

After a conversation with this "queer-looking little thing," who had her head shaved because of ringworm and was not permitted to attend school, Hudson decides he can appreciate her for her intelligence and "forget all about her freckles and nightcap."[57] When she asks him to return in five years to see her healed and more attractive, he reflects, "I fancy not, for at ten she would be self-conscious, and the loss would be greater than the gain." He explains that it is the "first instinctive impulses of the girl-child, combined with her imitativeness and wonderful precocity which make her so fascinating."[58]

In all his books Hudson's obsession with little girls comes through. Earliest, on his way to England he courts the nine-year old Honorina Marques, who interests him more than the passengers.[59] In *Far Away and Long Ago* he breathes life into the image of sensuous Anjelita galloping across the plains "bare-legged in her thin old cotton frock, her raven black hair flying loose behind," herself an emblem of unleashed nature.[60] In *Birds in Town and Village* the little girl who reveres wildlife "all at once pressed her two hands together" and "exclaimed rapturously, 'Oh, I do so love the birds!'" wins Hudson's heart forever.[61] There is no evidence that these relationships with children ever become sordid. Although they are courted and romanced, although they appear erotic, the little girls are kept at a distance from the narrator who employs them as examples of humanity actualizing its highest potential. Hudson repeatedly links childhood to the prelapsarian state, the existence prior to the split between man and nature. His relationships with little girls that he meets in travel and in the life of his books enable him to revisit, if but for a moment, this more perfect and spontaneous world.

Hudson also sought out youthful attributes in adults and tried to promote an appreciation of these in his readers. Typically the heroes and heroines are granted a prolonged childhood: Yoletta of *A Crystal Age* who first appears to be a little girl turns out to be a thirty-one year old woman; Rima, too, is initially perceived as a child not much taller than four feet and seven inches, close in height to Hudson's own wife, Emily. Paquíta, Lamb's bride of *The Purple Land* is "so small, so exquisite," that she comes across as pure impulsive youth.[62] In the essays, the country people, Mr. Flowerdew, or that shepherd of the down singing his way through the market place, all retain the qualities of youth. In the same vein, there are the adults who are admirable because they have the sense to worship children: the family in *Adventures Among Birds* abandons the heath because it reminds them of their deceased daughter, Violet, regarded as a flower-deity, and the "Old Man of Kensington Gardens" who "talks like one that's young" always strolls beside "a pretty little maid with locks of shiny gold."[63]

Ideal maturation is at its best a process that reverses itself: the individual that can wind back in time and relearn early sensations, impulses, and unclouded visions is moving toward the cultivation of a paradise within.

Other women in Hudson's books represent aspects of ever-changing Nature. The earth-beauty appears repeatedly in *The Purple Land* while Richard Lamb, an Englishman, journeys through the Banda Oriental. Despite a series of flirtations, Lamb ultimately remains faithful to his child wife waiting safely at home. The women framed by the South American wilds appear either helpless or stranded, fall instantly in love with the adventurer, or give him some pledge of undying loyalty. Although the women are intended to bring out the strength and heroism of Richard Lamb, they often become more fascinating than the protagonist himself. In the chapter, "Romance of the White Flower," we meet Dolores Zelaya, who nurses Lamb's wounds and creates "a subtler kind of fever in [his] veins—a malady not to be cured by fruit, fans or phlebotomy."[64] After a brief and platonic affair, Lamb resists her declaration of love by confessing, "I am not free—I have a wife," and rides off "thinking as she did, that [their] separation would be an eternal one."[65] Later, Lamb meets Demetria, who is bedecked in the "quaint" finery of the South American nobility and who is about to offer him marriage and wealth in exchange for her freedom from the oppressive and parasitic Don Hilario. His description of this woman is as detailed as his sketches of birds in his books on ornithology.

> She had on a grass-green silk dress, made in a fashion I had never seen before; extremely high in the waist, puffed out on the shoulders, and with enormous bell-shaped sleeves reaching to the elbows, the whole garment being plentifully trimmed with very fine cream-coloured lace. Her long, thick hair, which had hitherto always been worn in heavy plaits on her back, was now piled in great coils on her head and surmounted by a tortoise-shell comb a foot high at least, and

about fifteen inches broad at the top, looking like an immense crest on her head.[66]

Demetria is just one woman within the varied world of the Banda Oriental. Hudson attempts to cover a vast assortment of female characters—the submissive wives of Spanish origin, the exotic beauties, the peasant women, and the appealing victims in distress. Paquíta, Lamb's bride, is too good to be real: she obeys and waits like a Griselda; then, without jealousy, she embraces the destitute Demetria, a kind of competitor, and assists her husband in the rescue. For the most part, the women of *The Purple Land* become part of the earth, elements of the gaucho culture and background, embellishments of the lawless world.

Another female character that surfaces intermittently in Hudson's books is the guardian of Nature: she rebels against the view of human beings as rulers of the earth and demonstrates a love for all living things. It is possible that this character is based on Hudson's close friend and bird society colleague, Lady Grey, whom Violet Hunt describes quite vividly:

> [Hudson] spoke of a woman's 'passion' to me once, but it was only a spasm of humanitarianism evoked in the beautiful Dorothy Grey by the sight of an act of cruelty to a helpless animal. She noticed an ugly tramp picking a bird out of a hedge and putting it into his pocket. She rose from her seat. 'Give that to me!' she said, and the hedge thief, daunted by her splendid gesture, surrendered his prey; and the lady lay in Huddie's heart forever.[67]

Women engaged in preservationist activities appear in many forms in Hudson's books. If they are not variations on Lady Grey, they could be take offs on the woman Hudson recalls from his childhood. In *Far Away and Long Ago* Hudson looks back on a walk through the orchard with a group of adults who begin to panic and shriek at the sight of a snake and remembers the one woman who calmly saves the creature from a pointless death.

> One of the men, the first to find a stick or perhaps the most courageous, rushed to the front and was about to deal a killing blow when his arm was seized by one of the ladies and the blow arrested. Then, stooping quickly, she took the creature up in her hands, and going away to some distance from the others, released it in the long green grass, green in colour as its glittering skin and as cool to the touch. Long ago as this happened it is just as vivid to my mind as if it had happened yesterday.[68]

Hudson comments that this incident "bore fruit later" and "taught [him] to consider whether it might not be better to spare than to kill." Hudson's fictional women are often offshoots of this snake-charmer or bird-lover. Yoletta, a member of a purely vegetarian race, worships and protects the entire earth. Rima first dashes out of her hiding place to prevent Abel from hurling a stone at a serpent in her sacred wood.

> She had been watching my approach from some hiding-place among the bushes, ready no doubt to lead me a dance through the wood with her mocking voice, as on previous occasions, when my attack on the serpent caused that outburst of wrath. The torrent of ringing and to me inarticulate sounds in that unknown tongue, her rapid gestures, and above all her wide-open sparkling eyes and face aflame with colour, made it impossible to mistake the nature of her feeling.[69]

These guardians of Nature are almost pre-Eve women who live and move in gardens or orchards, who feel no instinctive enmity toward the serpent. They serve to remind us of Edenic harmony.

Another female character is the matriarch who in many ways bears resemblance to Hudson's own mother as she appears in *Far Away and Long Ago*. Hudson recalls "her sitting out of doors watching [their] sport with a smile, her book lying in her lap, and the last rays of the setting sun shining on her face."[70] Hudson explains his reactions to her death and then defines the immortality of maternal love: "a mother's love for the child of her body differs essentially from all other affections, and burns with so clear and steady a flame that it appears like the one unchangeable thing in this earthly mutable life, so that when she is no longer present it is still a light to your steps and a consolation."[71] Since Hudson argued that "the civilised woman—the artificial product of our self-imposed conditions—cannot have the same relation to her offspring as the uncivilised woman really has to hers," he often glorified women with families in the country, rustics who offered him hospitality during his travels, the mothers he remembers from his early life in South America.[72]

In *A Crystal Age*, the mother-worship is central. The utopia is governed by an omniscient matriarch, a set-up Yoletta tries to explain to the stranger who has been living in the house without any understanding of the government.

> Then suddenly, bursting into tears, she exclaimed; 'Oh, Smith, how could you be in the world and not know that there is a mother in every house? How could you travel and not know that when you enter a house, after greeting the father, you first of all ask to be taken to the mother to worship her and feel her hand on your head.[73]

Subsequently Yoletta leads Smith to the Queen Chastel where he first sees the statue of a woman with a "wistful face and silvery hair" which serves to preserve the memory of Mother Isarte who endured great suffering, the loss of her seven sons.[74] When Smith protests against this morbidity, the continual reminder of sorrow, Yoletta points out the unquestionable supremacy of the mother: "But she was a mother, Smith, do you understand? It would not be right for us to wish to have our griefs remembered for ever, to cause sorrow to those who succeed us; but a mother is different: her wishes are sacred, and what she wills is right."[75] Smith reflects upon this acceptance of a female deity: "her words surprised me not a little, for I had heard of infallible men, but never of women." The women in Hudson's books, particularly the utopian queen in *A Crystal Age*, appear all-knowing and in their capacity to comfort, heal, and see the future, resemble the powers of Nature herself.

Rima, Hudson's most famous creation, is the amalgam of all the qualities Hudson professed to admire: she reflects the beauty of the earth, the magic of childhood, the love of the guardian of Nature, and healing powers of motherhood. Rima, the spirit of Nature, appears to be a combination of bird and humanity, an ideal state. Abel, after asking himself why Rima has become so important to him, strains to describe her:

> Nothing so exquisite had ever been created. All the separate and fragmentary beauty and melody and graceful motion found scattered throughout nature were concentrated and harmoniously combined in her. How various, how luminous, how divine she was.[76]

Rima protects all the inhabitants within her sequestered woods. She mirrors the illusive quality of her surroundings. When indoors in Nuflo's cabin, she, like a chameleon, seems faded and subdued "like some common dull-plumaged little bird sitting listless in a cage."[77] In her natural habitat she is, however, the "living prismatic gem that changes its colour with every change of position."

It is not difficult to understand why some readers might feel impatient with Hudson's supernatural woman. For example, Hoxie Fairchild, who confesses to a "lively distaste for the bird-maiden," finds her "too avian to be human and too human to be preternatural, too unearthly to be a woman and too womanly to be a bird."[78] There is no doubt that at the turn of the century Rimas were becoming less popular. Rima does not pace the drawing room, entertain suitors, do needlework in a large armchair, or even study Latin: she refuses to conform to the growing penchant for realism. Instead she atavistically relates to the romantic dream vision, the *Alastor*-poet's goddess, Endymion's moon deity, or *La Belle Dame Sans Merci*. In keeping with this romantic genre, she is enshrouded in enough mystery to keep Abel's curiosity "continually active."[79] The secret of Rima's ancestry which sends Abel on that hazardous trek to Riolama also propelled several critics into a source hunt doomed to fail: J.V. Fletcher dates Rima back to Wordsworth's Lucy, Shelley's Cythna, and Meredith's girl in *Love in the Valley*;[80] Carlos Baker links Rima with the prophetess of Cashmire, Luxima, of Lady Morgan's *The Missionary* (1811);[81] Hoxie Fairchild believes that Hudson is indebted to Arthur O'Shaughnessey's *Colibri* (1881) whose heroine is an Indian girl also compared to a hummingbird; Rudolph Landry argues that Rima, the name at least, refers to "an anatomical structure in the larynx of a bird, the passage in the glottis between the vocal chords and the aretenoid cartilages."[82] Few of these source hunters trying to solve the riddle ever clearly define the spirit Rima was designed to represent or point to her many look-alikes in Hudson's other books. Rima bears similarity to Margarita of *The Purple Land*, who too appears as a being from a "far-off celestial region who had strayed to earth, just as a bird of white and azure plumage and unknown to our woods, sometimes appears, blown hither from a distant country or island, filling those who see it with wonder and delight."[83] Rima also resembles Margarita of *Far Away and Long Ago*, the family nurse with "large dark eyes and abundant hair" who died prematurely of consumption.[84] Rima shares characteristics with children and various birds scattered through Hudson's books. One thing is for sure: Rima is Hudson's most successful presentation of Nature in human form.

Yoletta is a similar, but weaker creation. She, the real daughter of Mother Chastel and next in line to take the throne, reflects Hudson's "vague faith in or hope of a better world."[85] Smith, the sometimes foolish Englishman in love with this fairy-like utopian, suggests man's appreciation of his own purer nature and the human yearning for perfection. His hosts, although repulsed by his crude speech and coarse garments, provide him with food, clothing and lodging. These people engage in ethereal chanting sessions, live only on vegetables, fruits, nuts, and honey, and share their leftovers with seemingly tame flocks of birds that swoop down onto the tables without fear. It is Smith's passion for Yoletta that moves him to learn the manners and customs of this alien culture which flourishes without machines, factories, money or strife. But Smith finds himself up against an impenetrable wall like Gulliver caught in the futility of striving to be one of the Houyhnhnms. Smith's fascination with this being who, like Rima, defies definitions, turns into a destructive obsession that brings on fever and depression. Yoletta's apparent lack of passion, her unattainability, only increases his despair. Smith exclaims, "How many men had been driven by love to such an end, and the women they had worshipped, and miserably died for, compared with Yoletta, were like creatures of clay compared with one of the immortals."[86] He acknowledges the fact that she is "a being of a higher order," and finds himself unable to unite with her or fully comprehend her race. Toward the close of the novel just before Mother Chastel is about to grant him his only wish, make him the new Father of the tribe and husband to Yoletta, Smith sabotages his own triumph. While reading the sacred volumes, he discovers what he considers to be a tragic secret, the utopian's incapacity to feel or even understand his kind of passion:

For the children of the house there could be no union by mar-

riage; in body and soul they differed from me: they had no
name for the feeling which I had so often and vainly declared;
therefore they had told me again and again that there was
only one kind of love, for they, alas! could experience one
kind only.[87]

When Smith realizes that Yoletta can "never be his, body and
soul," he drinks an elexir labeled "drink of me and be cured"
believing he will be instantly transformed into a being of "everlasting calm."[88] His haste brings about his death. In his last
moments Yoletta's shriek, indeed impassioned, multiplies and
fades; the reverberating cries resemble Nature's response to
the fall of man and woman:

> Then a great cry, as of one who suddenly sees a black phan-
> tom, rang out loud in the room, jarring my brain with the
> madness of its terror, and striking as with a hundred passion-
> ate hands on all the hidden harps in wall and roof; and the
> troubled sounds came back to me, now loud and now low,
> burdened with an infinite anguish and despair, as of voices of
> innumerable multitudes wandering in the sunless desolations
> of space, every voice reverberating anguish and despair; and
> the successive reverberations lifted me like waves and
> dropped me again, and the waves grew less and the sounds
> fainter, then fainter still, and died in everlasting silence.[89]

Characters like Yoletta and Rima are ephemeral. They are momentary gifts to the protagonists, Smith and Abel, who can
perceive them as the embodiments of avian grace, as true
representations of the ever-changing beauty of the earth. Their
desires to marry Yoletta and Rima are one and the same with
the human desire for pure communication and intimacy with
the soul of Nature. Because these women are spirits of Nature,
because they suggest our perfected selves, because they never
do seem real, their admirers can't sustain a communion with
them. The most disturbing and yet hopeful point in the plot of

both novels is that Abel and Smith come tantalizingly close to fusing with pure spirit.

Although most of Hudson's characters are idealized rustics or supernatural creations, *Fan: The Story of a Young Girl's Life* shows us that the naturalist was perfectly capable of presenting the people of London, the kind of characters that were a part of his immediate world. *Fan*, first published under the pseudonym of Henry Harford, was not well liked by the author himself or his reviewers: the *Athenaeum* said it is "as dull and badly put together as it is coarse and repulsive",[90] the *Spectator* admits that "it is immeasurably superior to the average product of the circulating libraries," but "in spite of its superiority, it is disappointing."[91] *Fan* is certainly not Hudson's best book or even a key to unlocking central themes, but it is significant because it opens up another side of its author. The characters live and breathe an urban reality: their relationships with the city, with each other, are complex, and in a sense, universal.

Fan, the heroine, born and bred in poverty and eventually adopted by Mary Starbrow, is the dullest person in the novel. She is Hudson's Pollyanna: really the long-lost daughter of an aristocrat, she possesses an innate grace and dignity that sets her aside from the vulgar masses. Fan is beyond sentimentalism: she lives for love alone: "for to her love was everything: 'all thoughts, all feelings, all delights' were its ministers and 'fed its sacred flame'; this was the secret motive ever inspiring her, and it was impossible for her to put any other, higher or lower, in its place."[92] Fan, with her apparent inability to feel passion, seems as removed and pre-fallen as the calm race of *A Crystal Age*. Hudson explains that her love was "not that sweet sickness and rage of the heart which is also called love, and which so enriches life that we look with a kind of contemptuous pity on those who have never experienced it, thinking that they have only a dim incomplete existence, and move through life ghost-like and sorrowful among their joyous brothers." Hers is that "purer, better affection which we prize as our most sacred possession, and even attribute it to the immortals." The novel consists of Fan proving her superiority again and again: she embraces Mary after each cruelty; she rescues Constance and Merton even after they desert and betray her; she forgives Captain Horton who kidnaps and attempts to rape her. Mary's critique of Fan best expresses Hudson's dissatisfaction with his own character:

> What are you made of, I wonder—are you merely a wax figure and not a human being at all? Once I imagined that you loved me, but now I see what a delusion it was; only those who can hate are able to love, and you are as incapable of the one as of the other.[93]

Certainly it is easier for a reader to accept inimitable humanity in the context of a romance within the exotic jungles of Venezuela than in the concrete environment of a newly industrialized London. Although the central character, herself, is weak and at times ridiculous, she becomes a foil that serves to bring forth the flaws and contradictions of the flesh-and-blood beings around her.

Fan contrasts most obviously with Mary Starbrow, one of the most alive and unpredictable people in all of Hudson's fiction. Fan first meets this "beautiful lady" when she, orphaned and starving, wanders the streets trying to survive as a step cleaner. We are introduced immediately to Mary's instability when her "sharp imperative tone" shifts suddenly to kindliness after perceiving the awe and worship in the pauper's eyes.[94] From this first encounter right up until the finale, Mary Starbrow oscillates from hot to cold, from rage to gentleness, from passion to hatred: she is "touchy, passionate, variable in tempers; and if her stormy periods were short-lived she also had cold and sullen moods, which lasted long and turned all her sweetness sour."[95] Hudson records through Fan's eyes every gesture, every recoil and sound within Mary's habitual eruptions. When Mary discovers Captain Horton's villainy the scene is as slow-motioned and detailed as one of the naturalist's descriptions of a snake about to strike. This is perhaps one of the finest temper tantrums in literature:

> She rose and paced the room, pausing at every step, and turning herself from side to side, like some savage animal, strong and lithe and full of deadly rage, but unable to spring, trapped and shut within iron bars. Her face changed to livid white, and looked hard and pitiless, and her eyes had a fixed stony stare like those of a serpent. And at intervals, as she moved about the room, she clenched her hands with such energy that the nails wounded her palms. And from time to time her rage would rise to a kind of frenzy, and find expression in a voice strangely harsh and unnatural, deeper than a man's and then suddenly rising to a shrill piercing key that startled Fan and made her tremble.[96]

In keeping with her pattern, this "strong, undisciplined woman," employs the young girl as a whipping post, a target for her sporadic tempests. In return for food, clothing, and shelter, she expects immediate forgiveness, unconditional love, and sustaining stability. Mary, known as a "great woman-hater—a kind of she-misogynist," makes repeated declarations of love to Fan, but the only kind of affection she is capable of is both inconstant and possessive.[97]

When Mary goes abroad, she selects a tutor whom she imagines will be a homely book-worm and no competition, a woman who will not replace her in Fan's heart. Before the actual meeting Mary tells Fan what she expects Constance Churton, the scholar, will look like: "the eyes are dim, no doubt, from much reading, and the nose long, straddled with a pair of spectacles and red at the end from dyspepsia and defective circulation."[98] When it turns out that Miss Churton defies this stereotype,

Mary warns Fan that if she transfers her love to this tutor, there will be a severe penalty. Mary sounds like a jealous husband threatening divorce:

> I don't want a divided affection, and I shall not share your affection with this woman, however beautiful and kind she may be; or rather, I shall not be satisfied with what is over after you have begun to worship her. . . . But I warn you, Fan, that if you ever transfer the affection you have felt for me to this woman, or this girl, then you shall cease to be anything to me. You shall be no more to me than you were before I saw you and felt a wish to take you to my heart; when you were in rags and half starved, and without one friend in the world.[99]

The inevitable comes to pass. Mary decides that Constance Churton has indeed stolen Fan and disowns the girl instantly and entirely. As is typical of Fan, she mourns the loss of the friendship more than the financial abandonment. Years later when Fan receives her income from her real father and endeavors to mend her breach with Mary, the autocrat still bears a grudge. Throughout the book this shaky relationship proceeds with Mary fluctuating between a passionate embrace and cold rejection.

Other characters in *Fan* are just as striking and three-dimensional. Constance Churton, the talented independent thinker, becomes increasingly suppressed and submissive under the influence of her husband, Merton, the hypocrite and glib rhetorician. Captain Horton, Mary's suitor, is not just a villain, but also has his share of virtue and shows some capacity for growth and reform. Arthur Eden, the aristocrat who fails to win Fan for his mistress, who disrespectfully propositions her and requests that she compromise herself, shows his honorable and generous side in his dealings with her after she has discovered that she is his long-lost half sister. These characters are not just symbols of perfection or emblems of evil; they are real, contradictory, complex. They prove that Hudson was capable of moving out of the romance and fantasy modes when he chose to do so.

Hudson's friends were repeatedly pointing out that the naturalist kept himself apart from the mortal world. They felt that even in social situations, Hudson distanced himself. Morley Roberts once said that "it's absurd for him ever to have married. Nature is his real and lasting love and any woman a mere incident."[100] What is seen as an idiosyncratic detachment is really the conscious effort on Hudson's part to rebel against what he saw as a turn-of-the-century tendency to inflate humanity. To Hudson, the human being was both part of and at one with Nature. Although his characters often appear dignified and distinct, they never eclipse his real subject, the large and all important backdrop of the universe.

Hudson had a habit of reminding his readers that all our human things are transitory. His most direct discussion of healthy detachment occurs in *Afoot in England* when Hudson talks about those who "lament the recent great change on Salisbury Plain," and the destruction brought about by war.[101]

> It is hateful to them; the sight of the camp and of troops marching and drilling, of men in khaki scattered about everywhere over a hundred square leagues of plain; the smoke of firing and everlasting booming of guns. It is a desecration; the wild ancient charm of the land has been destroyed in their case, and it saddens and angers them.

The narrator then veers away from the anticipated treatise by withdrawing his support: he says, "I was pretty free from these uncomfortable feelings," and then connects his own perspective with the attitude expressed in a Japanese legend:

> It is said that one of the notions the Japanese have about the fox—a semi-sacred animal with them—is that, if you chance to see one crossing your path in the morning, all that comes before your vision on that day will be illusion.

71

Hudson illustrates this belief by telling the story of a Japanese man who seeing a fox in the morning, "witnessed the eruption of Krakatoa, when the heavens were covered with blackness and kindled with intermitting flashes and the earth shaken by the detonations, and when all others, thinking the end of the world had come, were swooning with extreme fear, viewed it without a tremor as a very sublime but illusory spectacle."[102] Next Hudson becomes prescriptive and explains how anyone can attain this form of wise indifference.

> A somewhat similar effect is produced on our minds if we have what may be called a sense of historical time—a consciousness of the transitoriness of most things human—if we see institutions and works as the branches on a pine or larch, which fail and die and fall away successively while the tree itself lives for ever, and if we measure their duration not by our own few swift years, but by the life of nations and races of men. It is, I imagine, a sense capable of cultivation, and enables us to look upon many of man's doings that would otherwise vex and pain us, and, as some say, destroy all the pleasure of our lives, not exactly as an illusion, as if we were Japanese and had seen a fox in the morning, but at all events in what we call a philosophic spirit.

The wise Copernican pushes human affairs away from the nucleus of the universe. This means cultivation of the "philosophic spirit," and an awareness of the timeless force which reduces in importance all our institutions, wars, and pains.

Hudson believed that an individual could alleviate suffering by passing from the specific to the general, by absorbing the self in the vastness of the visible world. E. Preston Dargon, Hudson's acquaintance, once asked the author about the mental anguish of Abel after Rima's death: "What kept him from actual madness in his forest-hut?"[103] Hudson replied, "Nature, of course." The tormented lover, haunted by nightmares, does not become introverted or look to psychology for salvation.

The antidote is much simpler—a walk in the woods. Hudson believed that the growth of industry and the plague of urbanization were accompanied by a rise of subjectivism and egotism. The modern race encircled by machines, hazed in soot, had lost sight of a power beyond the self. For Hudson leaving the unnatural confines of the city was synonymous with breaking out of the bastille of selfhood. It is the full appreciation of Nature which leads to a deeper understanding of self, the real self, and which reveals to us our proper niche on earth. Once our stature is reasonably diminished, then pain too dwindles in intensity. An individual who finds beauty in the serpent, falls in love with the rare Hatta flower, detects an intermittent permanence in the flight of birds, frees the self, acknowledges Nature's infinitude, and cultivates the "philosophic spirit," the "fox-in-the-morning" perspective.

This pattern of moving from the self to the balm of vastness is demonstrated clearly by Smith's self-healing in *A Crystal Age*. After Smith is rejected by Mother Chastel, he dashes off to a "sequestered spot" where he can "indulge [his] resentful feelings."[104]

> I began to be affected by the profound silence and melancholy of nature, and by a something proceeding from nature—phantom, emanation, essence, I know not what. My soul, not my sense, perceived it, standing with fingers on lips, there, close to me; its feet resting on the motionless water, which gave no reflection of its image, the clear amber sunlight passing undimmed through its substance. To my soul its spoken 'Hush!' was audible, and again, and yet again, it said 'Hush!' until the tumult in me was still, and I could not think my own thoughts.[105]

This is Hudson's reciprocated pathetic fallacy: while he ascribes human traits to outdoor phenomena, Nature herself forces Smith to conform to her moods. The woods give him a temporary reprieve from his self-imposed depression:

All along the river a white mist began to rise, a slight wind
sprang up and the vapor drifted, drowning the reeds and
bushes, and wreathing its ghostly arms about the old trees:
and watching the mist, and listening to the 'hallowed airs and
symphonies' whispered by the low wind, I felt that there was
no longer any anger in my heart. Nature and something in
and yet more than nature had imparted her 'soft influences'
and healed her 'wandering and distempered child' until he
could no more be a 'jarry and discordant thing' in her sweet
and sacred presence.[106]

After communion with Nature, Smith overcomes his im-
pediments, pride and resentment, and finds the strength to
return to Yoletta and mend his breach with the Queen. He
dashes back to the house with a new feeling of "love and
sympathy for the suffering woman who had wounded [him]
with her unmerited displeasure." Intimacy with the soul of the
visible world brings him the self-knowledge and distance necessary for him to restore the relationship between himself and
his adopted society.

Hudson, who was a believer in occasional retreats, wrote
Morley Roberts, "Nature doesn't love us and we don't love Nature except in an indirect way. She stands proxy to the thing we
really love—our fellow creatures. She only comes in for the
over-flow."[107] As a novelist, Hudson demonstrates his own
aphorism: his creations receive enlightenment after periods of
seclusion in the wilds and return to civilization enriched with a
new and purer love. As a naturalist Hudson re-defines his vocation: "I have called myself a field naturalist for convenience'
sake, and chiefly because I do not exclude the non-human
world from my survey. A field naturalist is an observer of everything he sees—from a man to an ant or a plant."[108] This
statement is borne out by every book: his characters are always
a part of everything that exists.

CHAPTER IV

The Field Naturalist

EVEN AFTER *Green Mansions* made him a famous novelist, as Hudson explained to Ford Madox Ford, he did not like to be called an artist: "I'm not an artist. It's the last thing I should call myself. I'm a field naturalist who writes down what he sees."[1]

This vocation derives in part from Hudson's pronounced affiliation with the work of Gilbert White who in 1755 resigned his fellowship at Oriel College, Oxford, and settled as Curate at Selborne. White's retirement in Hampshire, spent in the observation of the local scene and in composition of letters to men of like interests, appealed to Hudson who himself glorified this withdrawal into rural simplicity. Hudson repeatedly declares himself akin to Gilbert White, whose *Natural History of Selborne* was given to him at age sixteen, just the "right thing to get for that bird-loving boy out on the pampas."[2] White's compilation of letters became for Hudson a holy writ to which he pays tribute in nearly every collection of out-of-door essays: in *A Hind in Richmond Park* Hudson claims that White in a letter to Daines Barrington supports his own ideas on music;[3] in *Nature in Downland* Hudson employs White's Letter LVI to express that "special quality" and "mental flavour" of the South Downs;[4] in *Adventures Among Birds* Hudson turns to White as

his authority on the sound of field crickets and ravens;[5] and
Hampshire Days reads as a testimonial to the Selborne Curate as
Hudson relates his own impressions on local churches and
Wolmer Forest, and grills his elderly landlady for more infor-
mation.[6]

Hudson's most extensive discussion of the early naturalist
occurs in *Birds and Man* where every detail of Selborne calls
forth his image. Hudson explains:

> I thought of White continually. The village itself, every fea-
> ture in the surrounding landscape, and every object, living or
> inanimate, and every sound, became associated in mind with
> the thought of the obscure country curate, who was without
> ambition, and was 'a still quiet man, with no harm in him--
> no, not a bit,' as was said by one of his parishioners.[7]

While wandering through the village, Hudson feels that
White's memory is "interwoven with living forms and sounds.[8]
He says, "It began to seem to me that he who had ceased to live
over a century ago, whose Letters had been the favourite book
of several generations of naturalists, was, albeit dead and gone,
in some mysterious way still living." This "continual sense of
an unseen presence" leads the narrator into a dialogue in which
he discusses the "marked difference in manner, perhaps in feeling between the old and new writers on animal life and nature."[9] Hudson perceives a modern disposition to emphasize
the more aesthetic and emotional aspects of nature. The new
naturalist is more than an amateur scientist collecting facts, but
he is a spiritualist with "a kind of subsidiary conscience, a
private assurance that in all [his] researches into the wonderful
works of creation, [he is] acting in obedience to a tacit com-
mand, or, at all events, in harmony with the Divine Will."[10]
Through assuming the first person plural, Hudson defines this
new breed of nature writers for the figuritive ghost of Selborne.

We are bound as much as ever to facts; we seek for them more and more diligently, knowing that to break from them is to be carried away by vain imaginations. All the same, facts in themselves are nothing to us: they are important only in their relations to other facts and things—to all things, and the essence of things, material and spiritual. We are not like children gathering painted shells and pebbles on a beach; but whether we know it or not, are seeking after something beyond and above knowledge.

This definition of a post eighteenth century naturalist who investigates all things "material and spiritual," who quests for unity in the universe, counters Hudson's other persona, the ordinary outdoor man with a professed interest in mere surfaces.

On one level, the more complex voice of W.H. Hudson is one of a field naturalist who is also a religious philosopher. His outdoor study brings about a mystical experience where the self merges with the ceaseless cycles of Nature and provides the soul with a sense of immortality, which for Hudson seemed far more tenable than the Christian after-life. On another level, the field naturalist is an artistic philosopher. Hudson emphasized the active relationship between the mind and Nature, one that results in mythmaking and the creation of metaphor which is central to both fiction and "science." Hudson saw art as the universal "instinct" to express beauty which in its highest form reflects the very spirit and breath of Nature. Hudson also believed that the true field naturalist transcends both the spheres of art and science: he is an individual independent of both and free to embrace the whole world as his subject matter.

Related to Hudson's definition of the field naturalist is his refusal to associate himself with any organized faith. In his letter to Morley Roberts of January 24, 1916, Hudson calls himself a "religious atheist" and describes a man who "should have gone into the army and that, he says, was his desire as a boy, but he was flung into the church and so he gets what satisfaction he can for his fighting instincts . . . as parson."[11]

Hudson deliberately distances himself from this parson and his wife.

> I wonder what he would say if he ventures to question me on my religious beliefs some day and I should reply that I'm a 'religious atheist!' The other day I was having tea with him and we got talking about Mysticism and I said that the mystics were all under a delusion. They looked at me and his wife seemed upset and so we dropped the dangerous topic.

In *Far Away and Long Ago* Hudson explores the dawning of his religious atheism. After his serious illness Hudson plunges into religious literature in an attempt to convince himself of the possibility of salvation. Once after reading Richard Baxter's *The Saint's Everlasting Rest*, the young naturalist, "assailed by lawless thoughts," finds himself envious of the "eternally damned."[12] This reaction, at the time seemingly blasphemous, eventually became the foundation for his mature philosophy.

> If an angel, or one returned from the dead, could come to assure me that life does not end with death, that we mortals are destined to live for ever, but that for me there can be no blessed hereafter on account of my want of faith, and because I loved or worshipped Nature rather than the Author of my being, it would be, not a message of despair, but of consolation; for in that dreadful place to which I should be sent, I should be alive and not dead, and have my memories of earth, and perhaps meet and have communion there with others of like mind with myself, and with recollections like mine.[13]

His hope for immortality of the soul drives the young Hudson into theology, sermons and meditations which only bring him more disputation and doubt. He claims, "The worst of it was that when I tried to banish these bitter, rebellious ideas, taking them to be the whisperings of the Evil One, as the books taught, the quick reply would come that the supposed Evil One was nothing but the voice of my own reason striving to make itself heard." Hudson describes his encounter with a neighboring gaucho who tells him that although he is supposedly a Roman Catholic and the Hudsons are Protestants, a minority considered to be heretics in that area of the world, there is really no difference since both orthodoxies are false:

> 'You see all this with your eyes,' he continued, waving his hands to indicate the whole visible world. 'And when you shut them or go blind you see no more. It is the same with our brains. We think of a thousand things and remember, and when the brain decays we forget everything, and we die, and everything dies with us.[14]

Although Hudson initially rejects the gaucho whom he feels is sadly deluded, in later life he returned to accept this view.

The clearest spokesman for Hudson's feelings about church establishments and the followers is the carpenter, Mr. Cawood, who in *Fan* sounds a great deal like the author's own "voice of reason." This man "known to be temperate, a good husband and father, and a clever industrious mechanic" is approached by the narrow-minded fanatic, Mrs. Churton, who arrives at his home to persuade him to save his soul and attend church.[15] Her lecture on the "truth of Christianity" culminates in advice—"to search the scriptures, to worship in public, and humbly seek instruction from our appointed teachers."[16] Cawood remains unmoved and heroically asserts his independence.

> I think we are free to do good or evil; and if there is a future life—and I hope there is—I don't think that anyone will be made miserable in it because he didn't know things better than he could know them. That's the whole of my religion, Mrs. Churton, and I don't think it a bad one, on the whole—for myself I mean; for I don't go about preaching it, and I don't ask others to think as I do.[17]

Once Cawood exempts himself from the debate over faith and turns to his own instinct as his authority, Fan, who is listening, feels "like a bird newly escaped from captivity." After months of enduring Mrs. Churton's tirades, Cawood's neutrality released her and spoke to "her disposition and humble intellect." The author apparently sides with Cawood and his saint-like heroine since the final speech of the carpenter sounds like Hudson's own voice.

> For here am I, neither for one thing nor the other. On one side are those who have the Bible in their hands, and tell us that it is an inspired book—God's word; on the other side are those who maintain that it is nothing of the sort; and when we ask what kind of men they are, and what kind of lives do they lead, we find that in both camps there are as good men as have ever lived, and along with these others bad and indifferent. . . . I thought it best to give it all up, and give my mind to something else.[18]

Hudson also abandoned the notion that there exists a Judge outside the self. Like the message Rima's apparition delivers to the nearly insane Abel, Hudson believed that people must grant their own peace and redemption.

> Think not that death will ease your pain, and seek it not. Austerities? Good works? Prayers? They are not seen; they are not heard, they are less than nothing, and there is no intercession. I did not know it then, but you knew it. Your life was your own; you are not saved nor judged; acquit yourself—undo that which you have done, which Heaven cannot undo—and Heaven will say no word nor will I.[19]

It is not until Abel realizes that Rima, the soul of Nature, endures as part of his own soul that he releases himself from guilt. He comes to see self condemnation for what it is—a cruelty worse than Rima's incendiary death: "for they had but tortured and destroyed her body with fire, while I cast this shadow on her soul—this sorrow transcending all sorrows, darker than death, immitigable, eternal."[20] Once he stops looking for forgiveness in the outside forces, he exorcises the fever from his brain and finds the "everlasting beauty and freshness of nature" completely restored.[21] Through Abel's revelations in *Green Mansions* Hudson shows how peace is attained through the awareness of a connection between the I and the infinite.

Hudson's spiritual communion with Nature comes alive in his letter to Morley Roberts, dated November 10, 1920.

> I never had such a sense of oneness, as when I was once on the Downs near Burlington Gap. It was a beautiful day, the sky was a deep wonderful blue, and before me there was a great spread of thinly growing viper's bugloss, such as I had seen on the pampa. It was so wonderful a sight that I *became* the blue of the sky and the bugloss and the air! Why I didn't seem to walk, I just floated, floated! Have you ever felt like that?[22]

This is what Hudson called the "natural mystical feeling" where the character or narrator himself attains this "oneness" with Nature. In *A Traveller in Little Things* Hudson defines this as the "perfect harmony," when the self extends into the surrounding space, and likens this event to spiritual revelation.[23]

> Sky and cloud and wind and rain, and rock and soil and water, and flocks and herds and all wild things, with trees and flowers—everywhere grass and everlasting verdure—it is all part of me, and is me, as I sometimes feel in a mystic mood, even as a religious man in a like mood feels that he is in a heavenly place and is a native there, one with it.

In these moments away from the artificiality of city life when he feels in tune with the earth, Hudson passes into this "mystic mood" where the surroundings become a part of and a reflection of the self. In his writings Hudson frequently echoes the scriptures to invest Nature with a religious significance: Smith of *A Crystal Age* compares the "translucence and splendour" of light filtering through the foliage to the effect of "stained glass in the windows of some darkening cathedral."[24] Abel, after a period of exile, returns to the Christian settlement like a prophet bringing new knowledge "of *his* world—the world of nature and of the spirit."[25]

At Selborne Hudson, conversing with the emanation of Gilbert White, brings up the ever evolving awareness of a unity in all living things as the central concern of the nineteenth century naturalist: "For we are no longer isolated, standing like starry visitors on a mountaintop, surveying life from the outside; but are on a level and part and parcel of it; and if the mystery of life daily deepens, it is because we view it more closely and with clearer vision."[26] The highest attainment for the new naturalist is this perception of an ongoing commensalism in Nature. The naturalist becomes like a priest imparting "not only the thing he sees but the spirit of his vision" and finally, his own relationship to it.[27]

Far Away and Long Ago contains two contrapuntal motifs which are in the end reconciled, one being the child's growing animistic relationship with all living things, the other, an increasing awareness of mortality threatening to tear young Hudson away from the delights in Nature. In the third chapter, Hudson remembers the response of his tutor to the death of the family dog: "That's the end. Every dog has his day and so has every man; and the end is the same for both. We die like old Caesar, and are put into the ground and have the earth shovelled over us."[28] This pronunciation throws Hudson into a depression which is temporarily alleviated by his mother's religious teachings. But the relief is interrupted by several other occurrences that keep "the thoughts and fear of death alive."[29] There are the semi-human cries of cattle being slaughtered, the visitor who almost perishes in the ravine, and the death of the young servant girl, Margarita. The theme climaxes near the close of the autobiography when sixteen year old Hudson is informed that because of his permanently injured heart, he could "drop down at any moment," a diagnosis which he feels is the obliteration of the entire universe.[30]

> This visible world—this paradise of which I had had so far but a fleeting glimpse—the sun and moon and other worlds peopling all space with their brilliant constellations, and still other suns and systems, so utterly remote, in such inconceivable numbers as to appear to our vision as a faint luminous mist in the sky—all this universe which had existed for millions and billions of ages, or from eternity, would have existed in vain, since now it was doomed with my last breath, my last gleam of consciousness, to come to nothing.[31]

Even the beauty of the outdoors could not ease these fears.

Hudson found in Nature, particularly "the autumnal migration," a mingling of two contrary sensations, "intense joy" and "ineffable pain."[32] Eventually as his health improved, he learned to accept the momentary pleasure derived from Nature as his peace. He explains at the close of his autobiography his decision to focus on happiness in the present tense.

> When I hear people say they have not found the world and life so agreeable or interesting as to be in love with it, or that they look with equanimity to its end, I am apt to think they have never been properly alive nor seen with clear vision the world they think so meanly of, or anything in it—not a blade of grass.[33]

Instead of continuing with his struggle to have faith in the possibility of an after-life, Hudson channeled his hopes for peace into this life. In *Far Away and Long Ago* he closes with a reaffirmation of life: "In my worst times, when I was compelled to exist shut out from Nature in London for long periods, sick and poor and friendless, I could yet always feel that it was infinitely better to be than not to be."[34]

It is characteristic of Hudson that in the midst of describing some natural phenomenon, he introduces the subject of death. Hudson came to believe that the encroachment of the end could intensify one's appreciation of Nature. In *Nature in Downland* he explains how the yearly decline of life can bestow on us a feeling of immortality.

> For these innumerable little lives quickly pass while ours endure. Futhermore, the brief life which they have is but one, and though their senses be brilliant they see not beyond their small horizons. To us the Past and the Future are open, like measureless countries of diversified aspect, lying beyond our horizon; yet we may see them and are free to range over them at will. It may even happen that the autumnal spectacle of the cessation of life on the earth, nature's yearly tragedy brought thus suddenly and sharply before the mind's eye, may cause us to realize for the first time what this freedom of the mind really means. It multiplies our years and makes them so many that it is a practical immortality.[35]

The mind observing cycles in Nature with this broad perspective will separate the self from the "innumerable" deaths and "all at once begin to abhor the sickly teachings of those who see in nature's mutations, in cloud and wind and rain and the fall of the leaf, and the going out of ephemeral life, nothing but mournful messages, dreary symbols, reminders of our mortality."[36] By detaching oneself from these minor cessations of life and instead by identifying oneself with the vernal rebirths, one can triumphantly cry, "I shall not die, but live!"

In the "Return of the Chiff-Chaff" the speaker demonstrates how he may turn to Nature for the sense of immortality. He begins by expressing his wish "to divest himself of himself—that second self which he has unconsciously acquired—to be like the trees and animals, outside of the sad atmosphere of human life and its eternal tragedy."[37] He feels haunted by images of departed friends, in particular, his wife, who brings about his somber mood: "The sweet was indeed changed to bitter, and the loss of those who were one with me in feeling appeared to my mind as a monstrous betrayal, a thing unnatural, almost incredible."[38] Hudson then traces his gradual return to peace through enchantment with Nature.

> Then little by little the old influence began to reassert itself, and it was as if one was standing there by me, one who was always calm, who saw all things clearly, who regarded me with compassion and had come to reason with me. "Come now," it appeared to say, "open your eyes once more to the sunshine; let it enter freely and fill your heart, for there is healing in it and in all nature. It is true the power you have worshipped and trusted will destroy you, but you are living to-day and the day of your end will be determined by chance only. Until you are called to follow them into that 'world of light,' or it may be of darkness and oblivion, you are immortal."[39]

The narrator animates Nature which appears in the form of a "mysterious mentor" advising him to immerse himself in the "unchanging call" of the Chiff-Chaff, a song from which the speaker separates himself, for "the small bird exists only in the present; there is no past, nor future, nor knowledge of death."[40] Once detached, the speaker finds relief from the "intolerable sadness—from the thought of springs that have been, the beautiful multitudinous life that has vanished." He realizes that his own moods are as mutable as the seasons and that "Nature herself in her own good time heals the wound she inflicts." He discovers that the power of his mind to project his loss even upon the resplendence of spring makes the disappearances of his loved ones seem less final: "They are not wholly, irretrievably lost, even when we cease to remember them, when their images come no longer unbidden to our minds. They are present in nature, through ourselves, receiving but what we give, they have become part and parcel of it and give it an expression."[41] In contrast, the loss serves to intensify the beauty once it is restored: "As when the rain clouds disperse and the sun shines out once more, heaven and earth are filled with a chastened light, sweet to behold and very wonderful, so because of our lost ones, because of the old grief at their loss, the visible world is touched with a new light, a tenderness and grace and beauty not its own." Hudson believed that our interactions with the visible world, our study of its ongoing life and death cycles, can help us see that our stay on earth is prolonged and can grant us a feeling of immortality.

In "A Boy's Animism," the heart of his account of his early years, Hudson recalls the shape and appearances of Nature evoking more powerful sensations than his mother's most profound religious teachings.

> These teachings did not touch my heart as it was touched and thrilled by something nearer, more intimate, in nature, not only in moonlit trees or in a flower or serpent, but, in certain exquisite moments and moods and in certain aspects of nature, in "every grass" and in all things, animate and inanimate.[42]

Hudson explains that this sense of "something" in Nature is due to "animism," a process defined at the start of the chapter: "by animism I do not mean the theory of a soul in nature, but the tendency or impulse or instinct, in which all myth originates, to *animate* all things; the projection of ourselves into nature."[43] This leads to the "sense and apprehension of an intelligence like our own but more powerful in all visible things.' In a chapter suggestive of Wordsworth's *Prelude*, Hudson traces the development of his "sense of the supernatural in natural things," a feeling which begins with the sensuous appreciation of the outdoors.[44]

Hudson recalls his first association with Nature as a physical delight—"the blue of the sky, the verdure of earth, the sparkle of sunlight on water, the taste of milk, of fruit, of honey, the smell of dry or moist soil, of wind and rain, of herbs and flowers."[45] This first appreciation is Edenic, a state prior to the infiltration of complex knowledge with its creative, spiritual and factual levels. Hudson describes a change in his eighth year when he became conscious of "something more than this mere childish delight in nature. . . . It was as if some hand had surreptitiously dropped something into the honeyed cup which gave it at certain times a new flavour."[46] Hudson defines a mystery tempered both with pleasure and fear, a feeling he found most powerful on late night rambles.

> Yet on the very next night I would steal out again and go to the spot where the effect was strongest, which was usually among the large locust or white acacia trees, which gave the name of Las Acacias to our place. The loose feathery foliage on moonlight nights had a peculiar hoary aspect that made this tree seem more intensely alive than others, more conscious of my presence and watchful of me.[47]

These early experiences of animism are equated with divine appearances—"similar to the feeling a person would have if visited by a supernatural being." Although the projection of the self onto Nature brings about the apprehension of a like intelligence, the force itself remains invisible, mute, indifferent. It stands "silent and unseen, intently regarding him, and divining every thought in his mind," yet takes "no visible shape nor speak[s] to him out of the silence." The imagination, of course, may grant this being a shape and a voice, but apart from the mind or the resultant myth, it remains a nebulous mystery.

Hudson distinguishes his animism from pantheism or superstition. Animism is the process underlying all nature worship, superstitions and myths, a faculty that expresses itself in the deification of the forces and laws of the universe: "This faculty or instinct of the dawning mind is or has always seemed to me essentially religious in character; undoubtedly it is the root of all nature-worship, from fetishism to the highest pantheistic development." In "The Quality of Whiteness," a chapter in *Idle Days in Patagonia*, Hudson argues that animism is independent of any one system of beliefs; it is a universal foundation for both primitive and civilized philosophies that perceive this living soul in Nature. Hudson sets himself apart from the anthropologists, Robertson, Smith, and Frazer, and speaks of Tyler who in his *Primitive Culture* uses the term to mean "a theory of life, a philosophy of primitive man, which has been supplanted among civilized people by a more advanced philosophy."[48] According to Hudson, "the mind's projection of itself onto nature, its attribution of its own sentient life and intelligence," is really a "primitive universal faculty on which the animistic philosophy of the savage is founded," one which hasn't been and cannot be extinguished.

> When our philosophers tell us that this faculty is obsolete in us, that it is effectually killed by ratiocination, or that it only survives for a period in our children, I believe they are wrong, a fact which they could find out for themselves if, leaving their books and theories, they would take a solitary walk on a moonlit night in the "woods of westermain," or any other woods, since all are enchanted.[49]

This "latent animism that is in all of us" manifests itself in various forms, from the sailor navigating a ship which he believes is "alive and intelligent" on a sea which is "no mere expanse of water, but a living conscious thing" to the types of tree-worship "found existing among a few of the inhabitants in some of the rustic villages in out-of-the-world districts in England."[50] But sometimes communion with Nature and a personification of the visible world results in the apprehension of a spirit which at times seems harshly indifferent to the human world. Hudson's description of the spirit of winter illustrates this seeming impersonality.

> There is no longer any recognition, any bond; and if we were to fall down and perish by the wayside, there would be no compassion: it is sitting apart and solitary, cold and repel-

ling, its breath suspended, in a trance of grief or passion; and although it sees us it is as though it saw us not, even as we see pebbles and withered leaves on the ground, when some great sorrow has dazed us, or when some deadly purpose is in our heart.[51]

Hudson's relationship with Nature based on the active link between the mind and the external world brings about the recognition of an Unseen Being along with a sense of its separation from the self, and at times, its lack of sympathy with the small human world.

In *Far Away and Long Ago* Hudson claims that he never lost this animistic faculty nurtured on the pampas. In fact, animism is a key to his books: in almost every work he includes the animistic experience of Nature in all its stages. Smith of *A Crystal Age* delights in the flight of buzzards and recalls "how often in former days when gazing up into such a sky, he had breathed a prayer to the unseen spirit."[52] In *Afoot in England* the narrator at Stonehenge describes "the unbedding of the lark," by animating the voices that "were not human nor angelic, but passionless," and by emerging from the experience with a sense of something other-worldly.[53] Rima, whose voice is both human and supernatural, becomes Hudson's most complete animistic creation, the imaginative embodiment of Nature.

For Hudson, poetic language is the outcome of the same process, the animistic activation of the visible world. Hudson specifically renames the process of making a metaphor as animistic excitement.

Let us remember that our poets who speak not scientifically but in the language of passion, when they say that the sun rejoices in the sky and laughs at the storm; that the earth is glad with flowers in spring, and the autumn fields happy; that the clouds frown and weep, and the wind sighs and "utters something mournful on its way"—that in all this they speak not in metaphor, as we are taught to say, but that in moments of excitement, when we revert to primitive con-

ditions of mind, the earth and all nature is alive and intelligent, and feels as we feel.[54]

In his own treatment of Nature, Hudson too shows us this
reversion to the "primitive condition of mind." In *A Little Boy
Lost* when Martin murders a spoonbill, he finds his own guilt
and remorse reflected in the very hues and shapes of the landscape.

> Swifter and vaster, following close upon the flying shadow,
> came the mighty cloud, changing from black to slaty grey;
> and then, as the sun broke forth again under its lower edge, it
> was all flushed with a brilliant rose colour. But what a
> marvellous thing it was, then the cloud covered a third of the
> wide heavens, almost touching the horizon on either side
> with its wing-like extremities; Martin gazing steadily at it,
> saw that in its form it was like an immense spoonbill flying
> through the air! He would gladly have run away then, to hide
> himself from its sight, but he dared not stir, for it was now
> directly above him; so, lying down on the grass and hiding his
> face against the dead bird, he waited in fear and trembling.[55]

Martin's own sense that he has committed a crime and his desire for punishment which has transformed the sky itself,
culminates in a "great cry of terror" from "all the wild birds."
Through Martin and his first transgression, Hudson not only
reveals the active relationship between mind and Nature, but
also demonstrates the workings of animistic mythmaking.

Hudson also finds a place for animism in his naturalist
writings and ornithology. In *Birds and Man* it takes the form of
a quest for human likenesses in nature:

> We have but to listen to the human tones in wind and water,
> and in animal voices; and to recognize the human shape in
> plant and rock, and cloud, and in the round heads of certain
> animals, like the seal; and the human expression in the eyes
> and faces, generally, of many mammals, birds and reptiles to
> know that these casual resemblances are a great deal to us.[56]

Hudson believed that emphasizing these resemblances to human beings could in its final impact express his vision of Nature and her workings with more accuracy. The best example occurs in *Birds in Town and Village* when a search for the wryneck, the source of a "strange penetrating call," modulates into a myth.[57]

> First heard as a bird-call, and nothing more, by degrees it grew more and more laugh-like—a long far-reaching, ringing laugh; not the laugh I should like to hear from any person I take an interest in, but a laugh with all the gladness, unction, and humanity gone out of it—a dry mechanical sound, as if a soulless, lifeless, wind instrument had laughed. It was very curious. Listening to it day by day, something of the strange history of the being, once but no longer human, that uttered it grew up and took shape in my mind; for we all have in us something of this mysterious faculty. It was not bird, no wryneck, but a being that once, long, long ago, in that same beautiful place, had been a village boy—a free careless, glad-hearted boy, like many another.

Leaving the bird behind, Hudson tells the tale of a child whose innocence is shattered by a too sudden awareness of death. This knowledge brings about extreme suffering and progressive deterioration until a spirit or witch introduces him to the antidote to mortality, a diet consisting solely of ants: "If any person should be able to overcome his repugnance to so strange a food so as to sustain himself on ants and nothing else, the effect of the acid on him would be to change and harden his flesh and make it impervious to decay or change of any kind. *He would, so long as he confined himself to this kind of food, be immortal.*"[58] After much anguish, the child adjusts to the new food and undergoes a Lamarckian transformation: "As his strength increased so did his dexterity in catching the small active insect prey; he no longer gathered the ants up in his palm and swallowed them with dust and grit, but picked them so deftly and conveyed them one by one to his mouth with lightning rapidity."[59] Hudson describes him after his many years of bodily adaptation as a "lean grey little man, clad in a quaintly barred and mottled mantle, woven by his own hands from soft silky material, and a close-fitting brown peaked cap on his head with one barred feather in it for ornament, and a small wizened grey face with a thin sharp nose, puckered lips, and a pair of round brilliant startled eyes."[60] After leading the reader away from the bird into the history of an odd man who haunts rural villages looking for ants, Hudson returns to the origin of his myth.

> I looked and beheld the thing that had laughed just leaving its perch on a branch near the ground and winging its way across the field. It was only a bird after all—only the wryneck; and that mysterious faculty I spoke of, saying that we all of us possessed something of it (meaning only some of us), was nothing after all but the old common faculty of the imagination.

Through the language of myth, a child's metamorphosis, Hudson communicates information about the voice, diet and habits of the real wryneck. This is not intended to be a sugar-coated deliverance of ornithological facts. Instead, Hudson hoped to express the feeling the creature excited in him, something he felt was as important as the facts. Hudson believed that the animistic faculty behind pantheism, hylozoism, nature-worship and behind the creation of Rima should also express itself in the work of a field naturalist. One who studies "the life and conversation of animals" has license to transform the wilds in order to reveal this consciousness and unity pervading all life.

What Hudson objected to most was specialization, the exclusive obedience to any one authority, and what he saw as the modern tendency to construct impenetrable boundaries between art and science. In "The Serpent in Literature" Hudson complains of the scientist who through his elaborate system of classification and nomenclature extinguishes the beauty and mystery of life.

> When the snakists of the British Museum or other biological workshop have quite done with their snake, have pulled it out of its jar and popped it in again to their hearts' content; weighed, measured, counted ribs and scales, identified its species, sub-species, and variety; and have duly put it all down in a book, made a fresh label, perhaps written a paper—when all is finished, something remains to be said; something about the snake; the creature that was not a spiral-shaped, rigid, cylindrical piece of clay-coloured gutta-percha, no longer capable of exciting strange emotions in us—the unsightly dropped coil of a spirit that was fiery and cold.[61]

This approach to the creature, one that is devoid of emotion, causes Hudson to direct his reader elsewhere for the more complete picture. "The poet does not see his subject apart from its surroundings, deprived of its atmosphere—a mere fragment of beggarly matter—does not see it too well, with all the details which become visible only after a minute and, therefore, cold examination, but as a part of the picture, a light that quivers and quickly passes, that we, through him, are able to see it too, and to experience the old mysterious sensations, restored by his magic touch."[62] After listing those who have caught the fear and magic of "snakiness"—Matthew Arnold, Gordon Hake, Shakespeare, Browning, Tennyson, Meredith, and Keats, the naturalist decides that Oliver Wendell Holmes's *Elsie Venner* is the "best presentation of serpent life" in prose because he views it "at a distance and as a whole, with the vision common to all men, and the artist's insight added."[63]

Hudson's praise of Holmes's treatment of the snake is consistent with his definition of the evolving field naturalist. Hudson informs the ghost of Gilbert White that modern books about Nature are moving in the "direction of a more poetic and emotional treatment of the subject."[64] Hudson demonstrates this approach in his own autobiography when he mingles his refutation of the notion of the serpent as mute with his memories from childhood.

> A long sibilation would be followed by distinctly-heard ticking sounds, as of a husky-ticking clock, and after ten or twenty or thirty ticks another hiss, like a long expiring sigh, sometimes with a tremble in it as of a dry leaf swiftly vibrating in the wind. . . . I, lying awake in my bed, listened and trembled. It was dark in the room, and to my excited imagination the serpents were no longer under the floor, but out, gliding hither and thither over it, with uplifted heads, in a kind of mystic dance.[65]

Also, in *Green Mansions* the serpent is both a real and imaginary creation, beautiful, enticing and yet suggestive of the fall.

> It was a coral snake, famed as much for its beauty and singularity as for its deadly character. It was about three feet long, and very slim; its ground colour a brilliant vermillion, with broad jet-black rings at equal distances round its body, each black ring or band divided by a narrow yellow strip in the middle. The symmetrical pattern and vividly contrasted colours would have given it the appearance of an artificial snake made by some fanciful artist, but for the gleam of life in its bright coils.[66]

In his books, both fiction and nonfiction, Hudson intertwines fact and emotion: he refuses to estrange any creature from its natural environment and imitate the enemies under attack in his campaign against "Feathered Women." Any creature without life, amputated from its habitat, could no longer activate the animistic faculty or excite the kind of imaginative soarings Hudson claims to experience on the downs: "I can almost realise the sensation of being other than I am—a creature with the instinct of flight and the correlated faculty; that in a little while, when I have gazed my full and am ready to change my place, I shall lift great heron-like wings and fly with little effort to other points of view."[67]

Although Hudson did attack the methods of the laboratory, he refrained from blaming science alone for the uglification of the wilds. Instead, he found a more general target, the tendency in both science and art to pull away from the earth. An artist whose excursions into a supernatural realm seem irreversible is as culpable as the scientist whose systems of classification make him lose sight of the magic and mystery within the real form in nature. The new field naturalist who makes room for emotion and fantasy may take imaginative flights in order to shed light on the actual scene, but should, like the bird, always return again to the ground. In *A Hind in Richmond Park* Hudson explains the importance of being in touch with the very essence of the object.

> Apart from the aesthetic feeling which the object or scene or atmospheric conditions may rouse, and from the sense of novelty, the lively interest we experience at times in what we see and smell and hear and feel, and from other things operating in us, there is a sense of the *thing itself*—of the tree or wood, the rock, river, sea, mountain, the soil, clay or gravel, or sand or chalk, the cloud, the rain, and what not—something, let us say, penetrative, special, individual, as if the quality of the thing itself had entered into us, changing us, affecting body and mind.[68]

In "A Serpent Mystery," a chapter of the autobiography, Hudson demonstrates his ideal approach, the transformation of the subject without loss of the "thing itself." He recounts his boyhood fascination with a unique black snake which appeared to be a "coal-black current flowing past [him]—a current not of water or other liquid but of some such element as quicksilver moving on in a rope-like stream."[69] He, in constant pursuit of this rarity, attributes to it human reactions and emotions: "The serpent might come upon me unawares and would probably resent always finding a boy hanging about his den."[70] In later life he unearths facts which partially explain the mystery of the ophidian's unusual color: "Eventually I heard of the phenomenon of melanism in animals, less rare in snakes perhaps than in animals of other classes, and I was satisfied that the problem was partly solved. My serpent was a black individual of a species of some other colour."[71] In this anecdote Hudson follows his own pattern: he describes the creature, analyzes the sensations evoked by it, animates it and then closes with the snake itself and a hypothesis informed by science.

Hudson remembers that as a boy he felt an almost inexplicable dissatisfaction with Gilbert White's *Selborne:* he sensed that something central to his own experience of Nature was missing.

> I read and re-read it many times, for nothing so good of its kind had ever come to me, but it did not reveal to me the secret of my own feeling for Nature—the feeling of which I was becoming more and more conscious, which was a mystery to me, especially at certain moments, when it would come upon me with a sudden rush. So powerful it was, so unaccountable, I was actually afraid of it, yet I would go out of my way to seek it. At the hour of sunset I would go out half a mile or so from the house, and sitting on the dry grass with hands clasped round my knees, gaze at the western sky, waiting for it to take me. And I would ask myself: what does it mean? But there was no answer to that in any book concerning the "life and conversation of animals."[72]

According to Hudson, the new naturalist is not only more mystical, more emotional, but also a rebel who refuses "to take one branch of life and give all his attention to that" and knows that "to specialise is to lose your soul."[73] To Hudson, this did not mean combining art and science or even attempting to reconcile seemingly disparate fields. He felt that real change can only come about when the artist and the scientist begin to feel "antagonistic" toward their respective niches and declare their independence of both.[74]

> If there are any signs of change, they are in the minds of those who are outside of the artistic world. And outside of the scientific world as well, seeing that in both cases the reflex effects of their vocation on their minds is to distort the judgment. I refer to those only who are outside both fields, whose reasoning and aesthetic faculties are balanced, whose interest is in the whole of life, and who have succeeded in preserving perfect independence of mind in a herd where those who have captured the first places dominate the others and impose their perverted judgments on them.[75]

The new naturalist should strive to transcend both the spheres of art and science, should work to be "untied, unconfined in a groove, free and appreciating his freedom, intensely interested in life in all its aspects and manifestations," and should aspire to worship Nature and imititate its infinitude.[76]

CHAPTER V

The Darwinist

SHORTLY AFTER HIS ILLNESS, Hudson read *The Origin of Species*, a book which was given to him by his brother, Edwin, who had just returned to South America after five years abroad. Hudson initially rejected Darwin: "When I had read and returned the book, and he was eager to hear my opinion, I said it had not hurt me in the least, since Darwin had to my mind only succeeded in disproving his own theory with his argument from artificial selection. He himself confessed that no new species had ever been produced in that way."[1] Edwin advised him to take a second look, to read the book again "as a naturalist."[2] After another examination, Hudson found that Darwin was beginning to alter his whole perception of Nature.

> And every creature I watched, from the great soaring bird circling the sky at a vast altitude to the little life at my feet, was brought into the argument, and was a type, representing a group marked by a family likeness not only in figure and colouring and language, but in mind as well, in habits and the most trivial traits and tricks of gesture and so on; the entire group in its turn related to another group, and to others still further and further away, the likeness growing less and less.[3]

Although the new doctrine modified his philosophy, he could

never accept Darwinism completely: he could never feel "wholly satisfied with natural selection as the only and sufficient explanation of the change in the forms of life."[4] Hudson integrated evolutionary theory with the Lamarckian notion that the environment could bring about structural changes in wildlife which were then passed on to the offspring.

Because Darwin had such a powerful influence over him, Hudson endeavored to challenge his ideas and distinguish himself from his predecessor. This pattern of attack began with a letter on January 28, 1870 to the Zoological Society of London in which he refuted Darwin's argument that the South American woodpecker, the Carpintero, had adapted itself to the pampas where there weren't any trees. Hudson's citing of several examples of the species in various shaded districts excited only a calm reply from Darwin himself who admitted the possibility of an error. Later in his books Hudson mentions Darwin in attempts to dispute his ideas. One favorite point of attack is Darwin's view that birds "possess an instinctive or inherited fear of man" which Hudson found "utterly erroneous."[5] Also, in his fiction, Hudson enjoyed portraying human beings, like Rima, who had intimate relationships with the avian race: "One arm was doubled behind her neck for her head to rest upon, while the other arm was held extended before her, the hand raised towards a small brown bird perched on a pendulous twig just beyond its reach."[6] Hudson believed that this communion between the human and the bird world was entirely possible. In *A Crystal Age* the whole society share their meals with flocks of wild birds that perch "quite fearlessly on the heads or shoulders of the company" and consume the leftovers from the banquet.[7]

Hudson not only defies Darwin's understanding of birds, but also reproaches him for having a limited insight into human nature. In *The Naturalist in La Plata* Hudson asserts his own supremacy as the authority on the psychology and speech patterns of the gaucho.

Darwin in his earlier years appears not to have possessed the power of reading men with that miraculous intelligence always distinguishing his researches concerning other and lower orders of beings. In the *Voyage of a Naturalist*, speaking of this supposed indolence of the gauchos, he tells that in one place where workmen were in great request, seeing a poor gaucho sitting in a listless attitude, he asked him why he did not work. The man's answer was that *he was too poor to work!* The philosopher was astonished and amused at the reply, but failed to understand it. And yet, to one acquainted with these lovers of brief phrases, what more intelligible answer could have been returned? The poor fellow simply meant to say that his horses had been stolen—a thing of frequent occurrence in that country, or, perhaps, that some minion of the Government of the moment had seized them for the use of the state.[8]

Such attempts to expose flaws in Darwin's work were forms of rebellion against one of the most dominant influences in his life. For one, Darwin helped Hudson make sense out of the contradictory elements he saw at work in Nature. In *Hampshire Days* when Hudson tries to present the "whole of life," he explains why we should learn to accept suffering: "The fact that as things are designed in this world of sentient life there can be no good, no sweetness or pleasure in life, nor any beauty or strength or lustre, nor any bright and shining quality of body or mind, without pain, which is not ancillary to life, but is involved in and a part of life, of its very colour and texture."[9] He illustrates this with the case of the baby robin ejected from its nest by the stronger cuckoo, an event in perfect accord with natural law: Hudson explains that this is Nature's means of keeping "her too rapidly multiplying creatures within bounds," and adds that "we, too, live in . . . that mysterious green world in which life and death and pleasure and pain are interwoven light and shade."[10] For Hudson, Darwin reinforced his own belief that a true representation of life must include pain and contest as well as pleasure and peace.

Darwinian thought also infiltrated Hudson's vision of utopia. In a letter to Garnett, Hudson attacks William Morris' *News From Nowhere* and calls it "childishly poor, so manifestly false" because the people are transformed into angels by the conception of "new social laws concerning the price of food and clothes and so on."[11] Hudson prefers his own utopic romance where evolution and time, not changes in the social order, perfect the race: "The sexual passion is the central thought in the *Crystal Age*: the idea that there is no millennium, no rest, no perpetual peace till that fury has burnt itself out, and I gave unlimited time for the change."[12] Smith, the central character and the epitome of human folly, walks right into the perfect world, but cannot be content: he is still too much of an animal to suddenly live like an angel. This is something he realizes right before his tragic annihilation when he knows that the chasm between himself and Yoletta, a higher order of being, can only be traversed by the plodding and seemingly eternal passage of time: he believes that the "passionless, everlasting calm" is due to the fact that these beings "had forever out lived, and left as immeasurably far behind as the instincts of the wolf and ape, the strongest emotion of which [his] heart [is] capable."[13] Hudson felt that a sudden change in the economic structure, or a revolution, or a new imposition of laws on the inhabitants of earth, were not answers or even steps in the right direction: they could not make Smith any more at home with his utopians.

Hudson hoped that the human race would evolve slowly and steadily toward perfection. *Green Mansions* more successfully than *A Crystal Age* shows the human being at various stages of evolution: the savages at the bottom of the ladder are close to beasts; Nuflo, Rima's guardian, although he too is carnivorous and at times resembles the savages, elevates himself because of his capacity to recognize and appreciate a being purer than himself. Of all the characters, Abel is the one that can most closely communicate with Rima, but like Smith, he is frustrated and finds himself incapable of learning her language. He also fails to live in complete harmony with Nature, to sustain himself on the vegetarian diet, or to exist for any length of time without strife or discord. After his shortlived romance with Rima who is at the apex and represents human potential, he returns to his civilization with a new knowledge of the real world and a conviction that with the passage of time people will move further away from their bestial beginnings and come closer to the purest spirit of Nature herself, become more like the Rima-race.

Hudson felt that Darwin's "great, almost self-evident truth" that "won a hearing in the world" was based on an unshaken faith in time as a continuum.[14] In a sense, *Far Away and Long Ago* is evolution applied to the individual: Hudson searches through his own memory, examines his struggles and adaptations within his past, and emerges with a clearer understanding of his present self. Darwin also provided Hudson with additional justification for personifying natural phenomena. Both the evolutionist and the animist perceive the link between lower forms of life and the human world. Both feel the great unity and commensalism that exist on earth. When Hudson claims there is a kinship between the musical impulse in insects and in human beings, he argues in support of animism and evolution at once:

> To the musical and artistic minded generally, this may seem an unpleasant idea, a degradation of art to something low and little. To the naturalist there is nothing low and little in this sense. But we know that the fact of evolution in the organic world was repellent to us for the same reason—because we did not like to believe that we had been fashioned mentally and physically out of the same clay as the lower animals.[15]

Hudson who from an early age experienced moments when Nature seemed to assume human forms, found in Darwin's community of descent a scientific ally.

Hudson often pressed the point that governmental change and the precarious relations amongst nations were minute particulars within a ceaseless flux. He liked to present himself as a man detached from political issues and events which he felt blocked us from seeing life as a whole. His position comes across clearly in several letters to Garnett whose preoccupation with politics moved him to express irritation:

> Why will you always introduce political remarks in your letters when as I've often said I'm not a politician and don't even look at anything of that sort in the newspaper I read? Thus on that subject we are not in the same world—or not on the same plane. Mine is the simple one, the uncomplex, and I live the life of Reason and common sense, but it is the lower sort of reason based on instinct—shelter, food, self-preservation and all that.[16]

In an effort to discourage Garnett from troubling him with current events, Hudson shifts from his usual stance of indifference to the unattractive derivation of Darwinism, the rationalization of war and destruction.

> You think it a "cursed war," I think it a blessed war. And it was quite time we had one for our purification and our [indecipherable] from the degeneration and rottenness which comes of everlasting peace. It was for this reason that I prayed for war in Ireland, which would have quickly spread to England, in those hateful days when the leaders of Liberalism—now clothed and in their right minds—were frantically jeering at Ulsterism. But this war is better, and the blood that is being shed will purge us of our detestable partisanship, our gross selfishness, and a hundred more. Let us thank the gods for a Wilhelm and a whole nation insane with hatred of England to restore us to health.[17]

It is difficult to reconcile this position with the voice of a humanitarian protesting against cruelty toward animals and with the ex-South American who was indeed familiar with the atroc-

ities of war since he in 1866 fought for a few months in the
Argentinian army against Paraguay. Even though this outburst
contradicts his other sentiments, it is very much consistent
with his belief that strife is central to growth and development.

In the final chapter of *A Hind in Richmond Park* Hudson
separates himself from the artistic world which to him seemed
as restlessly cyclical as the political world: "We see that this
question of art is in a perpetual state of flux. . . . We see groups
in rebellion against what they call conventional art: the very art
one knows in fact. These outbursts occur from time to time and
tend to grow more frequent. In a little while they die out, and
the generation that follows laugh at their folly. But again others
spring up to take their place."[18] Hudson prophesies a real
change in art which would not come about through the efforts
of any one movement, but rather through the underlying restlessness that makes all things evolve steadily toward their com-
pletion.

> Looking back, we see that they do and cannot lift art to a high
> plane. We see that art cannot progress: that on these lines and
> in that particular direction, it reached its highest level ages
> ago. But the only explanation of these futile attempts is the
> sense of dissatisfaction with art generally, which every indi-
> vidual, young or old, with an alert progressive mind comes to
> in his own life. The revolt against "conventional art," even
> when it results in something we laugh at, is a sign of progress
> towards something above the arts, which will satisfy the crea-
> tive powers, the desire of self-expression.[19]

The questions posited at the close of *A Hind in Richmond Park*
are purposely left unanswered: "What then would take the
place of art, all the world made in a certain form, if art should
die out? How would the sense of beauty, and the desire to express emotion that it creates, be expressed at last?" Possibly
Hudson envisions a new form of expression as ethereal as
Rima's warbling or as mystical as the chants of the Crystal Age

utopians that are "low, tremulous, and AEolian in character, wandering over the entire room as if walls and ceiling were honeycombed with sensitive musical cells answering to the deeper vibrations."[20] Hudson believed that art's replacement would be as illusory and as various as Nature herself.

This hope for progress toward something above and beyond art is another manifestation of Hudson's protest against boundaries. Along with this dream of forging a new means of creative expression and a new vocation beyond both art and science, Hudson took great pains to avoid being categorized himself. For Hudson, true freedom meant commingling seemingly diverse fields, expanding the scope of the field naturalist to encompass the "whole wide world," and also avoiding the dictatorship of any one predecessor. H. J. Massingham is partly correct when he claims that Hudson's independence alienated the average reader who found it "difficult to come to terms with a man who is neither one thing nor the other, but both in one, a oneness that is specifically neither."[21] It was Hudson's aim to reflect and imitate the very indefinability and infinitude of Nature that led to some misconceptions about him as a man and the misunderstanding of his work which often prevents readers from exploring beyond the popular *Green Mansions*.

Notes

CHAPTER I

1. For articles concerned with the "Rima" controversy, see Marjory Stoneman Douglas, "W. H. Hudson: Monuments to His Green World," *The Carrell*, Vol. 15 (1974) 1–16; Roger Fry, "The Hudson Memorial," *The Dial*, 79 (November 1925), 370–3; Hominy Mowbray, "Rhymes on Rima," *The Literary Digest*, 88, Jan. 1926, p. 36; H. B. "A Colonial's Rima," *The Literary Digest*, 86 (8 Aug. 1925), p. 23.

2. *GM*, 90.

3. *GM*, 91-2.

4. *CA*, 12.

5. *NLP*, 203. The text reads "not more impossible."

6. *NLP*, 104.

7. Herbert S. Gorman, *The Procession of Masks* (Boston: B. J. Brimmer Co., 1923), p. 111.

8. Richard Aldington, "The Prose of W. H. Hudson," *The Egoist*, I (15 May 1914), p. 186.

9. Ford Madox Ford, *Portraits From Life* (Boston: Houghton Mifflin Co., 1937), p. 49.

10. Edward Thomas, *A Literary Pilgrim In England* (London: Methuen & Co., Ltd., 1917), p. 190.

11. *HRP*, 318.

12. H. J. Massingham, "Centenary of W. H. Hudson," *Nature*, CXLVIII (16 August 1941), p. 188.

13. John Galsworthy, "Foreword" in *FAR*, vii.

14. Edward Garnett, "W. H. Hudson: An Appreciation," *The Academy and Literature*, LXII (21 June 1902), p. 633.

15. *HD*, 38.

16. *ROB*, 1–2.

17. *ROB*, 25.
18. *ROB*, 16–7.
19. Ford Madox Ford, *Thus to Revisit: Some Reminiscences* (New York: Octagon Books, Inc., 1966), p. 68.
20. The elipsis is in Ford's essay and does not represent an omission.
21. Ford Madox Ford, "W.H. Hudson," *The American Mercury*, XXXVII (March 1936), p. 309.
22. Ibid., p. 306.
23. Ibid., p. 310.
24. Violet Hunt, "The Death of Hudson," *The English Review*, XXXVI (January 1923), pp. 23 & 28.
25. Ibid., p. 36.
26. "Cunninghame Graham and W. H. Hudson," *The Living Age*, 351 (September 1936), p. 66.
27. See A. F. Tschiffely, *Don Roberto: Being the Account of the Life and Works of R. B. Cunninghame Graham, 1852–1936* (London: William Heinemann Ltd., 1937), p. 436. Graham composed the Prologue to *Allá Lejos Y Hace Tiempo* (Buenos Aires: Jocabo Pueser, 1945), a translation by Fernando Pozzo and Celia Rodrigues de Pozzo. Pozzo also translated *A Hind in Richmond Park, Una Cierva En La Parque De Richmond* (Buenos Aires: Editorial Claridad, 1944). W. H. Hudson has also been translated into Chinese, Czech, Danish, Dutch, Estonian, Finnish, French, German, Greek, Hebrew, Italian, Japanese, Portuguese, Russian, Servian, Swedish, Thai and Turkish. A list of translations is included in John R. Payne, *W. H. Hudson: A Bibliography* (Hamden, Connecticut: Archon Books, 1977), pp. 213–222.
28. See *The Living Age*, pp. 66–7.
29. R. B. Cunninghame Graham, "W. H. Hudson Memorial," *Nature*, 110 (23 December 1922), p. 846.
30. Ezra Pound, "Hudson: Poet Strayed into Science," *The Little Review*, VII (May-June, 1920), p. 13.
31. Ibid., p. 16.
32. Ibid., p. 13.
33. Ibid., p. 17.
34. Ibid., p. 13.
35. Harold Goddard, *W. H. Hudson: Bird-Man* (New York: E. P. Dutton & Co., 1928), p. 16.

CHAPTER II

1. See Frank M. Chapman, "William Henry Hudson . . . American,"

Audubon Magazine, XLV (September-October, 1943), p. 269.

2. William Henry Hudson, *Diary*, p. 28.
3. Ibid., p. 29.
4. Ibid., p. 34.
5. *ROB*, pp. 14–15.
6. *ROB*, p. 39.
7. Morley Roberts says in *ROB*, p. 21 that he met Hudson in 1880. See C.M. Brack, Jr. and James J. Hill, Jr., "Morley Roberts' First Meeting with W.H. Hudson," *English Literature in Transition* (1880–1920); 18 (1975), pp. 36–37. They find a letter from Roberts to Edward Garnett that suggests the meeting took place in the winter of 1879.
8. From Roberts' letter to Garnett in Brack and Hill's note.
9. *ROB*, p. 27.
10. *MBB*, p. 52.
11. *FAN*, p. 289.
12. *FAN*, p. 335.
13. *MBB*, p. 148.
14. *MBB*, p.p. 40–1.
15. *FAR*, p. 298.
16. *FAR*, p. 300.
17. *FAR*, p. 302.
18. *FAR*, p. 304.
19. *EO*, p. 255.
20. Printed in *LBL*, pp. 149–54.
21. *FAN*, p. 1.
22. *FAN*, p. 7.
23. *FAN*, p. 21.
24. *FAN*, p. 25.
25. *AIE*, pp. 33–4.
26. *SL*, p. 22.
27. *MBB*, p. 79.
28. *MBB*, p. 85.
29. *ND.*, p. 18.
30. *HD.*, pp. 47–8.
31. *AIE*, p. 179.
32. *AIE*, pp. 179–80.
33. *SL*, p. 43.
34. See *ROB*, p. 198.

35. *LE*, pp. 291–2.
36. *LE*, p. 294.
37. *LE*, pp. 301–2.
38. *AAB*, p. 39.
39. *ND*, pp. 255–6.
40. *DMP*, p. 311.
41. *ND.*, p. 258.
42. *HD*, p. 113.
43. *HD*, p. 114.
44. *HD*, pp. 114-5
45. Herbert Faulkner West, ed., *Two Letters on the Albatross* (Hanover, New Hampshire: Westholm Publications, 1955).
46. *DMP*, p. 249.
47. *DMP*, p. 320.
48. *DMP*, p. 322.
49. *DMP*, p. 103.
50. *DMP*, pp. 119–20.
51. *CA*, p. 225.
52. *BLP*, pp. 120–30.
53. *IDP*, p. 4.
54. *ROB*, p. 128.
55. See *MBB*, pp. 193-4; for more information about Hudson's Last Will and Testament, see Herbert Faulkner West, *For a Hudson Biographer* (Hanover, New Hampshire: Westholm Publications, 1958), pp. 28–9.
56. *MBB*, p. 23.
57. *ND.*, pp. 2–3.
58. *HD.*, p. 46.
59. *HD.*, p. 129.
60. *LE*, pp. 9–10.
61. *FAR*, pp. 3–4.
62. *CA*, p. 17.

CHAPTER III

1. *MBB* , 119.
2. William Rothenstein, "Genius at the Turn of the Century," *Atlantic Monthly*, 149 (February 1932), p. 236.
3. Ford Madox Ford, "W. H. Hudson," *The American Mercury*, XXXVII (March 1936), p. 315.

4. Violet Hunt, *I Have This To Say: The Story of My Flurried Years* (New York: Boni & Liveright, 1926; reprinted AMS Press, 1982), p. 30.

5. Violet Hunt, "The Death of Hudson," *The English Review*, XXXVI (January 1923), p. 26.

6. *AIE*, 25–6.

7. Ford Madox Ford, *Portraits From Life* (Boston: Houghton, Mifflin Co., 1937), pp. 54–6.

8. *TLT*, 201–2.

9. Violet Hunt, *The English Review*, p. 31.

10. *MBB*, 292–3.

11. Edward Garnett, "Introduction" in *GAR*, p. 3.

12. Ibid., p. 4.

13. *MBB*, 166. For more information on the friendship between Hudson and Thomas see John Moore, *The Life and Letters of Edward Thomas*, (London: William Heinnemann Ltd., 1939), p. 129.

14. "Preface" to *Cloud Castle* reprinted in *DMP*, 315–6.

15. *MBB*, 42.

16. *MBB*, 238-9.

17. Ford, *Portraits From Life*, p. 52.

18. *MBB*, 347–8.

19. *GAR*, 103–4.

20. *FAR*, 13.

21. *FAR*, 14.

22. *FAR*, 26.

23. *FAR*, 43.

24. *FAR*, 140–1.

25. *FAR*, 161.

26. *FAR*, 164.

27. *FAR*, 177; 180.

28. *FAR*, 264.

29. *FAR*, 191.

30. *FAR*, 192.

31. *HD*, 301.

32. *HD*, 302–3.

33. *AIE*, 19.

34. *AIE*, 21–2.

35. *AIE*, 23.

36. *AIE*, 24.

37. *AIE*, 29.
38. *AIE*, 31.
39. *AIE*, 31–2.
40. *SL*, 30.
41. *SL*, 32.
42. *GM*, 129.
43. *IDP*, 98–9.
44. *IDP*, 100.
45. *IDP*, 97.
46. *IDP*, 101–2.
47. *LBL*, 130–1.
48. *LBL*, 74.
49. See Henry Chester Tracy, "Hudson as Mutant," *The Adelphi*, Vol. II (August 1924), pp. 216–23.
50. *TLT*, 117.
51. *TLT*, 120.
52. *TLT*, 121.
53. *TLT*, 125–6.
54. *TLT*, 113.
55. *TLT*, 115.
56. *TLT*, 129.
57. *TLT*, 133.
58. *TLT*, 110.
59. W. H. Hudson, *Diary Concerning His Voyage From Buenos Aires to Southhampton On the Ebro* (Hanover: Westholm Publications, 1958), pp. 25–6.
60. *FAR*, 151.
61. *BTV*, 5.
62. *PL*, 4.
63. The poem is printed in *LBL*, 171–200.
64. *PL*, 164.
65. *PL*, 198; 201.
66. *PL*, 291–2.
67. Violet Hunt, *The English Review*, pp. 26–7.
68. *FAR*, 219–20.
69. *GM*, 85–6.
70. *FAR*, 11.
71. *FAR*, 329–30

72. *FAR*, 12.
73. *CA*, 130–1.
74. *CA*, 142.
75. *CA*, 143.
76. *GM*, 144.
77. *GM*, 108.
78. Hoxie N. Fairchild, "Rima's Mother," *PMLA*, LXVIII (1953), p. 357.
79. *GM*, 144.
80. James V. Fletcher, "The Creator of Rima: W. H. Hudson: A Belated Romantic," *Sewannee Review*, XLI (January 1933), 24–40.
81. Carlos Baker, "The Source Book for Hudson's *Green Mansions*," *PMLA*, LXI (1946), 252–7.
82. Rudolph J. Landry, "The Source of the Name 'Rima' in 'Green Mansions,'" *N & Q* (December 1956), 545–6.
83. *PL*, 172–3.
84. *FAR*, 44.
85. *CA*, v.
86. *CA*, 176–7.
87. *CA*, 235.
88. *CA*, 236.
89. *CA*, 246.
90. *Athenaeum*, 16 (July 1892), p. 92.
91. *Spectator*, 27 (August 1892), p. 296. Also see A. J. H., "W. H. Hudson, 'Henry Harford' and the Story of *Fan*," *The Bookman's Journal & Print Collector*, VIII (July 1923), 109–12.
92. *FAN*, 207.
93. *FAN*, 483.
94. *FAN*, 44–5.
95. *FAN*, 81.
96. *FAN*, *140*.
97. *FAN*, 89.
98. *FAN*, 161.
99. *FAN*, 170–1.
100. *ROB*, 259–60.
101. *AIE*, 242.
102. *AIE*, 242–3.
103. E. Preston Dargon, "Rambles with W. H. Hudson," *The New Republic*, XXVII (13 July 1920), p. 190.

104. *CA*, 138.
105. *CA*, 138–9.
106. *CA*, 140.
107. *MBB*, 174.
108. *HRP*, 322.

CHAPTER IV

1. Ford Madox Ford, "W. H. Hudson," *The American Mercury*, XXXVII (March 1936), p. 314.
2. *FAR*, 338.
3. *HRP*, 302.
4. *ND*, 21–2.
5. *AAB*, 140–1; 253.
6. *HD*, 184; 210; 205–6.
7. *B&M*, 238.
8. *B&M*, 239.
9. *B&M*, 240 & 243.
10. *B&M*, 243–4.
11. *MBB*, 153–4.
12. *FAR*, 319
13. *FAR*, 319–20.
14. *FAR*, 323.
15. *FAN*, 228.
16. *FAN*, 232.
17. *FAN*, 234–5.
18. *FAN*, 233–4.
19. *GM*, 335.
20. *GM*, 336.
21. *GM*, 341.
22. *ROB*, 179.
23. *TLT*, 244–5.
24. *CA*, 139–40.
25. *GM*, 4.
26. *B&M*, 245.
27. John Galsworthy, "Foreword" in *GM*, viii.
28. *FAR*, 35.
29. *FAR*, 43.

30. *FAR*, 316.
31. *FAR*, 317–8.
32. *FAR*, 339–40.
33. *FAR*, 347.
34. *FAR*, 348.
35. *ND*, 196.
36. *ND*, 197.
37. *TLT*, 201.
38. *TLT*, 202.
39. *TLT*, 202–3.
40. *TLT*, 203–4.
41. *TLT*, 205.
42. *FAR*, 244.
43. *FAR*, 235.
44. *FAR*, 237.
45. *FAR*, 238.
46. *FAR*, 238–9.
47. *FAR*, 242–3.
48. *IDP*, 310. Also see *ROB*, 130.
49. *IDP*, 111.
50. *IDP*, 113; *FAR*, 246.
51. *IDP*, 112–3.
52. *CA*, 222.
53. *AIE*, 245.
54. *IDP*, 111.
55. *LBL*, 13.
56. *B&M*, 111.
57. *BTV*, 41.
58. *BTV*, 45.
59. *BTV*, 46.
60. *BTV*, 47.
61. *BN*, 180.
62. *BN*, 183.
63. *BN*, 186 & 189.
64. *B&M*, 246–7.
65. *FAR*, 217–8.
66. *GM*, 84–5.

67. *ND*, 26–7.
68. *HRP*, 33–4.
69. *FAR*, 227.
70. *FAR*, 229.
71. *FAR*, 231.
72. *FAR*, 338–9.
73. *HRP*, 319.
74. *HRP*, 317.
75. *HRP*, 317–8.
76. *HRP*, 319.

CHAPTER V

1. *FAR*, 343.
2. *FAR*, 344.
3. *FAR*, 345.
4. *FAR*, 346.
5. *BTV*, 147.
6. *GM*, 33–4.
7. *CA*, 40.
8. *NLP*, 347.
9. *HD*, 26.
10. *HD*, 27–8.
11. *GAR*, 236.
12. *GAR*, 237.
13. *CA*, 235.
14. *FAR*, 346.
15. *HRP*, 276.
16. *GAR*, 281.
17. *GAR*, 201–2.
18. *HRP*, 322.
19. *HRP*, 323.
20. *CA*, 101–2.
21. H.J. Massingham, "Centenary of W.H. Hudson," *Nature* 148 (August 16, 1941), p. 188.

Bibliography

PRIMARY SOURCES

The Collected Works of W. H. Hudson. 24 Volumes, New York: E. P. Dutton & Co., 1923 (Reprinted, AMS Press, 1968.)

Hudson, William Henry. *Green Mansions: A Romance of the Tropical Forest*. New York: Alfred A. Knopf. 1916.

Letters from W. H. Hudson, 1901–1922. Ed. Edward Garnett. New York: E. P. Dutton & Co., 1923.

Letters on the Ornithology of Buenos Ayres. Ed. David R. Dewar. Ithaca, New York: Cornell University Press, 1951.

Men, Books and Birds. Ed. Morley Roberts. London: Eveleigh, Nash & Grayson, Ltd., 1925.

Two Letters on an Albatross. W. H. Hudson & R. B. Cunninghame Graham. Introduction by Herbert Faulkner West. Hanover, New Hampshire: Westholm Publications, 1955.

W. H. Hudson's Letters to R. B. Cunninghame Graham. Ed. Richard Curle. London: Golden Cockerel Press, 1941.

William Henry Hudson's Diary Concerning his Voyage from Buenos Aires to Southampton on the Ebro. Notes by Jorge Casares. Hanover, New Hampshire: Westholm Publications, 1958.

SECONDARY SOURCES

A. J. H. "W. H. Hudson, 'Henry Harford,' and the Story of *Fan*." *Bookman's Journal and Print Collector*, VIII (July 1923), 109–112.

Aldington, Richard. "The Prose of W. H. Hudson." *The Egoist*, I (15 May 1914), 186–7.

Antología de Guillermo Enrique Hudson Con Estudios Críticos Sobre su Vida y su

Obra. Por Fernando Pozzo, E. Martínez Estrada, Jorge Casares, Jorge Luis Borges, H. J. Massingham, V. S. Pritchett y Hugo Manning. Buenos Aires: Editioral Losada, S. A., 1941.

Ara, Guillermo. *Guillermo E. Hudson: El Paisaje Pampeano y su Expresión*. Buenos Aires, Ministerio de Educación: Universidad de Buenos Aires, 1954.

The Athenaeum. A review of *Fan*. No. 3377 (16 July 1892), p. 92.

"Avian Clairvoyance of a Bird-Like Genius." *Current Opinion*, LXVI (January 1919), 46–7.

Baker, Carlos. "The Source-Book for Hudson's *Green Mansions*," PMLA, LXI (1946), 252–7.

Baldwin, Stanley. *On England and Other Addresses*. New York: Frederick A. Stokes Company, 1926, pp. 126-9.

Barfield, Owen. *Saving the Appearances: A Study in Idolatry*. New York: Harcourt Brace Jovanovich, 1957.

Bennett, Arnold. *Books and Persons: Being Comments on a Past Epoch, 1908–1911*. New York: George H. Doran & Company, 1917, pp. 278–9.

Bird-Lore. An Appreciation of W. H. Hudson. XXIV (November-December, 1922), 362.

Brack, O M, Jr. and James J. Hill, Jr. "Morley Roberts' First Meeting with W. H. Hudson." *English Literature in Transition (1880–1920)*, 18 (1975), 36–7.

Brickell, Herschel. "W. H. Hudson, Bridge-Builder Between the Americas." *Saturday Review of Literature*, XXVI (10 April, 1943), pp. 11–2.

Broca, Brito. "W. H. Hudson, Ciência e Poesia." *Cultura Política: Revista Mensa de Estudos Brasilieros*. lll (Juno 1943), 181–6.

Brock, A. Clutton. "William Henry Hudson." *The Times Literary Supplement*, 24 (August, 1922), p. 542.

Cahoon, Herbert. "Herman Melville & W. H. Hudson," *American Notes and Queries*, VIII (December 1949), 131–2.

Canby, Henry Seidel. *Definitions: Essays in Contemporary Criticism*. New York: Harcourt, Brace & Co., 1924, pp. 166–74.

Chapman, Frank M. "William Henry Hudson . . . American." *Audubon Magazine*, XLV (September-October, 1943), 264–9.

Charles, Robert H. "The Writings of W. H. Hudson." *Essays & Studies by Members of the English Association*, XX (1935), 135–51.

"A Colonial's 'Rima.'" *The Literary Digest*, 86 (8 August 1925), 23.

Colton, A. "The Quality of W. H. Hudson," *Yale Review*, VI (July 1917), 856–8.

Conrad, Joseph. *Last Essays*. New York: Doubleday, Page & Co., 1926, pp. 136–7.

Cunninghame Graham, R. B. *The Conquest of the River Plate*. New York: Doubleday Page & Co., 1924, pp. 1–8.

Cunninghame Graham, R. B. "W. H. Hudson Memorial." *Nature*, 110 (23 December 1922), 846.

"Cunninghame Graham and W. H. Hudson," *The Living Age*, 351 (September 1936), 65–7.

Curle, Richard. *Caravansary and Conversation: Memories of Places & Persons*. New York: Frederick A. Stokes Co., 1937, pp. 181–93.

_____. "W. H. Hudson." *Fortnightly Review*, CXVIII (October 1922), 612–9.

Cutright, Paul Russell. *The Great Naturalists Explore South America*. New York: The Macmillan Co., 1940, pp. 33–7.

D. "W. H. Hudson," *Notes & Queries*, 194 (5 March 1949), 104.

Dargon, E. Preston. "Rambles with W. H. Hudson." *The New Republic*, Vol. XXVII (July 13, 1921), 188–90.

De La Mare, Walter. *Pleasures and Speculations*. London: Faber & Faber, Ltd., 1940, pp. 55–6.

Dewar, David R. "W. H. Hudson's First Days in England." *Notes and Queries*, 204 (February 1959), 57–8.

_____. "W. H. Hudson's Visit to Ireland." *Notes & Queries*, 205 (May 1960), 188.

Douglas, Marjory Stoneman. "W. H. Hudson: Monuments to his Green World." *The Carrell*, 15 (1974), 1–16.

E. R. "The Work of W. H. Hudson." *English Review*, II (April 1909), 157–64.

Espinoza, Enrique. "La Reconquista de Hudson." *Revista Hispànica Moderna* (Enero y Abril, 1944), 86–99.

_____. *Tres Clásicos Ingléses de la Pampa: F. B. Head, William Henry Hudson, R. B. Cunninghame Graham*. Santiago de Chile: Babel, 1951.

Estrada, Ezequiel Martínez. *El Mundo Maravilloso de Guillermo Enrique Hudson*. Buenos Aires: Fondo de Cultura Económica, 1951.

_____. "Estetica y Filosofía de Guillermo Enrique Hudson." *Revista Hispánica Moderna* (Julio y Octobre, 1944), 299–306.

Evans, C. S. "Writings of W. H. Hudson." *The Bookman* (N.Y.), LII (September 1920), 18–21.

Fairchild, Hoxie. "Rima's Mother." *PMLA*, LXVIII (1953), 357–70.

Fletcher, James V. "The Creator of Rima; W. H. Hudson: A Belated Romantic." *Sewanee Review*, XLI (January 1933), 24–40.

Ford, Ford Madox. *Portraits From Life*. Boston: Houghton Mifflin Co., 1937, pp. 38–56.

_____. "Three Americans & a Pole." *Scribner's Magazine*, XC (October 1931), 379–86.

_____. *Thus to Revisit: Some Reminiscences*. New York: Octagon Books, Inc., 1966, pp. 68–78.

_____. "William Henry Hudson," *The American Mercury*, XXXVII (March 1936), 306–17.

_____. "William Henry Hudson: Some Reminiscences." *The Little Review*, VII (May-June, 1920), 1–12.

Franco, Luis. "Hudson en La Pampa." *Revista Hispánica Moderna* (Enero y Abril, 1944), 99–106.

Frederick, John T. *William Henry Hudson*. New York: Twayne Publishers, Inc., 1972.

Fry, Roger. "The Hudson Memorial." *The Dial*, 79 (November 1925), 370–3.

Gallo, Antonio. "El Gaucho Descubridor de Traplanda." *Revista Hispánica Moderna* (Julio y Octobre, 1944), 306–8.

_____. "Hudson y lo Nacional." *Revista Hispánica Moderna* (Julio y Octobre, 1944), 308–11.

_____. "Nuevos Testimonios Sobre G. E. Hudson." *Revista Hispánica Moderna* (Enero y Abril, 1944), 106–10.

_____. "Un Epistolario Reminiscente de Hudson." *Revista Hispánica Moderna*. (Enero y Abril, 1944), 110–112.

Galsworthy, John. *Candelabra: Selected Essays & Addresses*. New York: Charles Scribner's Sons, 1933, pp. 264–9.

_____. "Four Novelists in Profile." *The English Review*. 55 (November, 1932), 485–500.

Garnett, Edward. *Friday Nights: Literary Criticisms & Appreciations*. London: First Series, The Traveler's Library, 1929, pp. 23–39.

_____. "The Genius of W. H. Hudson." *The Literary Digest International Book Review*, I (December 1922), 23.

_____. "W. H. Hudson." *The Dial*, LXII (February 9, 1917), 83–7.

_____. "William Henry Hudson: An Appreciation." *The Academy & Literature*, LXII (21 June 1902), 632–4.

Goddard, Harold. *W. H. Hudson: Bird-Man*. New York: E. P. Dutton & Co., 1928.

Gorman, Herbert S. *The Procession of Masks*. Boston: B. J. Brimmer & Co., 1923, pp. 107–22.

Hamilton, Robert. "The Spirit of W. H. Hudson: An Evaluation," *Quarterly Review*, CCLXXV (October 1940), 239–48.

_____. *W. H. Hudson: The Vision of Earth*. London: J. M. Dent & Sons

Ltd., 1946.

Harper, George McLean. "Hardy, Hudson, Housman." *Scribner's Magazine*, LXXVIII (August 1925), 151–7.

————. *Spirit of Delight*. London: Ernest Benn Ltd., 1928, pp. 70–91.

Haymaker, Richard E. *From Pampas to Hedgerows & Downs: A Study of W. H. Hudson*. New York: Bookman & Associates, 1954.

Hellyar, Richmond H. "The Late W. H. Hudson." *Spectator*, 130 (6 January 1923), 16–17.

Hewlett, Maurice. *Extemporary Essays*. London: Oxford University Press, 1922, pp. 13–6.

Hilton, Ronald. "Recuerdos de un Criollo: William Henry Hudson." *Bulletin of Spanish Studies*, XXV (January 1948), 19–26.

Hind, Charles Lewis. *More Authors & I*. London: John Lane, The Bodley Head Ltd., 1922, pp. 141–6.

Hubbard, Sara A. "Nature by Down and Pave." *The Dial*, XXIX (1 September 1900), 120–122.

"Hudson and Blunt." *The New Republic*. Fall Literary Supplement (27 September 1922), 113–4.

Hudson en Quilmes y Chascomus. Estudio, selección y notas de Alcides Degiuseppe. Buenos Aires: Ministerio de Educación, Subsecretaria de Cultura, 1971.

Hudson, Julia G. "Concerning W. H. Hudson's Family." *The Literary Digest International Book Review*, I (December 1922), 77.

Hughes, Merrit Y. "A Great Skeptic: W. H. Hudson." *University of California Chronicle*, XXVI (April 1924), 161–74.

"Human Naturalist." *The Outlook*, 132 (13 September 1922), 54.

Hunt, Violet. "The Death of Hudson." *The English Review*, XXXVI (January 1923), 23–5.

————. *The Flurried Years*. London: The Camelot Press, Ltd., 1926.

————. *I Have This to Say: The Story of my Flurried Years*. New York: Boni & Liveright, 1926. (Reprinted AMS Press, 1982.)

James, William. *Talks to Teachers on Psychology: And To Students on Some of Life's Ideals*. New York: Henry Holt & Co., 1902, pp. 258–264.

Kelly, Florence Finch. "Silver Grey Laurels: An Appreciation of W. H. Hudson." *The Bookman* (N.Y.), XLV (March 1917), 84–8.

Kramer, Hilton. "Patagonia Revisited." *The New York Times Book Review*. 30 July 1978, pp. 3 & 16.

Landry, Rudolph J. "The Source of the Name 'Rima' in 'Green Mansions.'" *Notes and Queries* (December 1956), 545–6.

Lockley, R. W. "Guillermo Enrique Hudson." *Nosotros*, 14 (Julio de 1941), 52–8.

Looker, Samuel. "W. H. Hudson & Richard Jefferies," *Notes and Queries*, Vol. 194 (30 April 1949), 195–6.

Massingham, H. J. "The Art of W. H. Hudson." *The Living Age*, XXVII (7 October 1922), 51–3.

———. "The Centenary of W. H. Hudson." *Nature*, CXLVIII (16 August 1941), 187–9.

———. "W. H. Hudson." *The London Mercury*, III (November 1920), 73–81.

———. "W. H. Hudson." *The Nation & The Athenaeum*, XXXI (26 August 1922), 708–9.

Maurice, Arthur. "The Birds' Best Human Friend—W. H. Hudson." *The Mentor*, 12 (August 1924), 21–5.

Mendoza, Angélica. "Guillermo Enrique Hudson (1841–1922)." *Revista Hispánica Moderna*. (Julio y Octobre, 1944), 193–222.

——— & William Tindall. "Two Views of Hudson, Genius of the Pampas." *The New York Times Book Review* (December 7, 1941).

Moore, John. *The Life and Letters of Edward Thomas*. London: William Heinemann Ltd., 1939.

Mowbray, Hominy. "Rhymes on Rima." *The Literary Digest* (N. Y.), 88 (16 January 1926), 34.

Mumford, Lewis. *The Story of Utopias*. New York: The Viking Press, 1962, pp. 173–6.

The Nation. An Appreciation of W. H. Hudson. CXV (13 September 1922), 241.

Nicholson, E. M. "Birds in a Village." *Cornhill Magazine*, LIX (July 1925), 24–35.

Nicholson, Max. *The Environmental Revolution: A Guide for the New Masters of the World*. New York: McGraw Hill Book Company, 1970.

"Our Belated Recognition of the Greatest Living Writer of Outdoor Literature." *Current Opinion*, 60 (May 1916), 349–50.

Payne, John R. *W. H. Hudson: A Bibliography*. Hamden, Connecticut: Archon Books, 1977.

Peter, G. Earle. "William Henry Guillermo Enrique Hudson." *Razón y Fábula* (Bogotá), 12 (1969), 63–7.

Phelps, William Lyon. "The Mystery and Charm of W. H. Hudson." *The Literary Digest International Book Review*, I (December 1922), 13.

Pound, Ezra. "Hudson: Poet Strayed into Science." *Little Review*, VII (May-June, 1920), 13–7.

"A Priest of Nature's Oracles." *Current Opinion*, 73 (November 1922), 648.

Pritchett, V. S. "W. H. Hudson: The Naturalist of La Plata," *The Geographical Magazine*. XIII (August 1941), 188–97.

Reid, Forrest. *Retrospective Adventures*. London: Faber & Faber, 1941, pp. 110–23.

Rhys, Ernest. "W. H. Hudson: A Rare Traveller." *Nineteenth Century*, LXXXVIII (July 1920), 72–78.

Roberts, Morley. "W. H. Hudson." *Cornhill Magazine*, 69 (October 1930), 406–18.

———. "W. H. Hudson." *Virginia Quarterly Review*, VI (October 1930), 507–21.

———. *W. H. Hudson: A Portrait*. New York: E. P. Dutton & Co., 1924.

Rodker, John. "W. H. Hudson." *The Little Review*, VII (May-June, 1920), 18–28.

Roosevelt, Theodore. "An Introductory Note," W. H. Hudson, *The Purple Land*. New York: E. P. Dutton & Co., 1916, pp. ix–x.

Rosenbaum, Sidonia C. "William Henry Hudson: Bibliografía." *Revista Hispánica Moderna* (Julio Y Octobre, 1944), 222–30.

Rothenstein, William. "Genius at the Turn of the Century." *Atlantic Monthly*, 149 (February 1932), 233–43.

———. *Since Fifty: Men & Memories, 1922–1938; Recollections of William Rothenstein*. New York: The Macmillan Co., 1940, pp. 6–8.

Salt, Henry S. "W. H. Hudson, As I Saw Him." *Fortnightly Review*, CXIX (February 1926), 214–24.

Schneeman, Peter. "Pound's 'Englischer Brief': A Look Toward Germany." *Paideuma*, 7 (1978), 309–16.

Schumaker, Wayne. *English Autobiography, Its Emergence, Materials & Form*. Berkeley: University of California Press, 1974.

Senet, Rodolfo. "Las Mujeres de la Tierra Purpurea." *La Prensa*, Sección Segunda (Marzo 17 de 1929).

Shrubsall, Dennis. *W. H. Hudson: Writer and Naturalist*. Tisbury, Wiltshire: The Compton Press Ltd., 1978.

The Spectator. "Recent Novels:" A Review of *Fan*. 27 August 1892, p. 296.

Squire, J. C. *Life & Letters*. London: Hodder & Stoughton Ltd., 1917, pp. 11–7.

Storer, Robert W. "Letters on the Ornithology of Buenos Ayres." *The Auk*, 68 (July 1951), 389–90.

Swinnerton, Frank. *The Georgian Scene: A Literary Panorama*. New York: Farrar & Rinehart, 1934, pp. 140–6.

Thomas, Edward. *A Literary Pilgrim in England*. London: Methuen & Co., Ltd., 1917, pp. 190–9.

Thomas, W. Beach. "The Hudson Centenary." *Fortnightly Review*, 156 (August 1941), 163–9.

Titsworth, Paul Emerson. "William Henry Hudson, 'A Traveller in Little

Things.'" *The South Atlantic Quarterly*, XXII (April 1923), 166–70.

Tomalin, Ruth. *W. H. Hudson*. London: H. F. & G. Witherby Ltd., 1954.

Tracy, Henry Chester. "Hudson As Mutant." *The Adelphi*, II (August 1924), 216–23.

Tschiffely, Aimé F. *Don Roberto: Being the Account of the Life & Works of R. B. Cunningham Graham: 1852–1936.* London: William Heinemann Ltd., 1937.

Van Doren, Mark. "W. H. Hudson. *The Nation*. Fall Book Supplement, CXV (October 1922), 373–4.

Warren, C. Henry. "Introduction," Richard Jefferies, *The Story of My Heart*. London: Eyre and Spottiswoode, 1949, pp. v–xvi.

Wells, Carlton F. *The G. M. Adams-W. H. Hudson Collection*. Ann Arbor: William C. Clements Library, 1943, Bulletin 39.

West, Herbert Faulkner. *For a Hudson Biographer*. Hanover, New Hampshire: Westholm Publications, 1958.

_____. *W. H. Hudson's Reading*. Privately printed, 1947.

Weygandt, Cornelius. *Tuesdays at Ten: A Gathering From The Talks of Thirty Years on Poets, Dramatists & Essayists*. Philadelphia: University of Pennsylvania Press, 1928, pp. 255–77.

White, Georgia Atwood. "Lost—An American." *The Bookman*. (N. Y.), LXIX (July 1929), 490–4.

Williams, Harold. *Modern English Writers: Being A Study of Imaginative Literature, 1890–1914*. London: Sidgwick & Jackson Ltd., 1925, pp. 347–8.

Wilson, G. F. *A Bibliography of the Writings of W. H. Hudson*. London: *The Bookman's Journal*, 1922.

_____. "W. H. Hudson As An Explorer." *The Bookman's Journal and Print Collector*, VII (January 1923), 111–2.

Woodward, E. L. "W. H. Hudson." *The Spectator*, 1 August 1941, p. 105.

Woolf, Leonard. *Essays on Literature, History, Politics, etc.* New York: Harcourt Brace & Company, 1927, pp. 72–80.

Worthing Cavalcade: William Henry Hudson, A Tribute By Writers. Ed. Samuel J. Looker. Worthing: Aldridge Bros., 1947.

INDEX

INDEX

INDEX